# CRIMINAL (IN)JUSTICE

## WHAT THE PUSH FOR DECARCERATION AND DEPOLICING GETS WRONG AND WHO IT HURTS MOST

## RAFAEL A. MANGUAL

CENTER
STREET®

NASHVILLE · NEW YORK

Center Street
Hachette Book Group
1290 Avenue of the Americas, New York, NY 10104
centerstreet.com
twitter.com/centerstreet

Originally published in hardcover and ebook by Center Street in July 2022
First trade paperback edition: July 2023

Center Street is a division of Hachette Book Group, Inc. The Center Street name
and logo are trademarks of Hachette Book Group, Inc.

The publisher is not responsible for websites (or their content) that
are not owned by the publisher.

The Hachette Speakers Bureau provides a wide range of authors for speaking
events. To find out more, go to hachettespeakersbureau.com or email
HachetteSpeakers@hbgusa.com.

Center Street books may be purchased in bulk for business, educational, or
promotional use. For information, please contact your local bookseller or the
Hachette Book Group Special Markets Department at special.markets@hbgusa.com.

Print book interior design by Timothy Shaner, NightandDayDesign.biz

Library of Congress Control Number: 2022938336

ISBNs: 9781546001522 (trade paperback), 9781546001539 (ebook)

Printed in the United States of America

LSC-C

Printing 1, 2023

Praise for

# CRIMINAL (IN)JUSTICE

"In *Criminal (In)Justice*, Rafael Mangual draws on the seemingly forgotten lessons of our past success to make a powerful (and timely) case against discarding the systems and approaches that brought about the remarkable decline in crime that began in the early 1990s. This admirable and highly informed departure from the conventional wisdom about criminal justice in the United States is required reading for those concerned about public safety."

—William Barr, former US attorney general and bestselling author of *One Damn Thing after Another: Memoirs of an Attorney General*

"Rebuilding trust between the police and communities of color—who disproportionately suffer the impact of crime—requires honesty, understanding, and bravely following the facts wherever they lead. Everyone who cares about the quality of life in America's most dangerous zip codes has a duty to read this book even if it makes them uncomfortable."

—Bill Bratton, ret. commissioner, NYPD, chief, LAPD, and author of *The Profession: A Memoir of Community, Race, and the Arc of Policing in America*

"For years, elite voices have insisted that the greatest threat to minority communities is a racist criminal justice system and that decarceration and depolicing are the best way to save black and brown lives. In *Criminal (In)Justice*, Rafael Mangual steeps himself in the data to expose this narrative about race, crime, and justice as dangerously false—and he offers a better way forward."

—Megyn Kelly, journalist and host of *The Megyn Kelly Show* and #1 *New York Times* bestselling author of *Settle for More*

"To be considered enlightened on incarceration in our times is to learn certain glum mantras suggesting a pitilessly bigoted system America ought be ashamed of. Rafael Mangual is a bearer of truth, which almost always reveals these gloomy tenets as distortions and outright falsehoods. Take heart from his teachings, and work to change the world with knowledge rather than agitprop."

—John McWhorter, bestselling author of *Woke Racism: How a New Religion Has Betrayed Black America*

"Rafael Mangual has done America a great public service. In this elegantly written, carefully researched book, he explains our exploding crime problem: how we got ourselves into it and how we can get ourselves out. If there's a more important issue than this, I don't know what it is."

—Dennis Prager, nationally syndicated radio talk show host, cofounder of PragerU, and author of *The Rational Bible: Deuteronomy.*

To the victims of criminal injustices
across the country,
and to my children, who I hope
inherit a safer world.

# CONTENTS

# CRIMINAL
# (IN)JUSTICE

# WHY "CRIMINAL (IN)JUSTICE"

During the summer of 2019, I was sitting in my office and scrolling through one of my social media feeds when I came across one of the most tragic videos I had ever seen.[1] The harrowing footage was leaked to the public shortly after being captured by a Chicago Police Department surveillance camera that had been set up in the Austin neighborhood on the city's West Side. It showed a light-colored sedan slowly approaching a small group of people standing near the sidewalk of a residential street. In that group stood a young woman—just 24 years old—named Brittany Hill. In her arms was her one-year-old daughter. The little girl, perhaps thinking the slowing car was occupied by friends or family, waved at the vehicle. Within seconds, the vehicle's two occupants opened fire. The two men with Hill at the time of the shooting dashed out of harm's way, while Hill turned to shield her daughter before trying to get away herself. The video shows Hill limping away from the assailants before collapsing onto the pavement, with her daughter still clinging to her. Hill managed to drag herself and her daughter behind the bumper of a parked car and heroically threw herself over her little girl, not knowing if the gunmen would continue their barrage. One of the men that was standing with Hill reentered the frame with a firearm in hand shortly after the shooters drove off. He hopped into a black Mercedes-Benz and gave chase. As Brittany Hill writhed on the street, two men drove up in another car, got out, and lifted her limp body off the ground and into the backseat of their car. Hill's one-year-old could be seen sitting up on the asphalt and watching the men loading her mom into the vehicle before trying to use her not-yet-mastered ability to walk in order to get to her mother. The video ended just as another man picked the little girl up as her mother was driven off to a local hospital, where she was pronounced dead shortly after arriving.

Because the shooting was captured by a police surveillance camera, officers were able to track down and arrest two suspects within hours. Thirty-nine-year-old Michael Washington, according to news reports, was out on parole at the time of the shooting, after serving time for a drug charge. Citing prosecutors, the *Chicago Sun-Times* reported that "Washington has nine felony convictions, including for a 2004 second-degree murder charge and a 2001 battery charge that was reduced from attempted murder in a plea agreement."[2] Twenty-three-year-old Eric Adams, the second alleged shooter, was reported to have been out on probation at the time of the shooting, following a conviction for aggravated unlawful use of a weapon in 2018. In addition to the gun offense, Adams's Chicago police record includes arrests for public-order offenses relating to marijuana possession and gambling.

It's my experience that most fair-minded people who hear or read a story like this inevitably end up wondering the same thing: What on earth were these guys—*especially Washington*—doing out on the street? A guy with priors gets convicted of aggravated unlawful use of a weapon, and all he gets is *probation*, while a guy with *nine* prior felony *convictions* (not to mention God knows how many arrests)—two of which involved murder and attempted murder—gets paroled before he's 40? From where I was sitting, the fact that these two men were free on the morning Brittany Hill was killed was outrageous. It was also incongruous with what so many criminal justice reform advocates have been saying for as long as I've been following these issues.

Unfortunately, Hill's is just one of countless stories of lives lost, of flesh torn up, and of trauma suffered because the criminal justice system failed to incapacitate repeat offenders who have made their refusal to live within the bounds of the law clear many times over. Stories like hers—those of heinous and serious crimes perpetrated by repeat offenders who could have been, but weren't, behind bars at the time—illustrate what this book means by "criminal (in)justice."

In post-2020 America, critiquing the inefficiencies and inequities—which most certainly exist—in the American criminal justice system (while there are technically thousands of systems in the US, I use the singular simply because it is a widely accepted colloquialism) isn't just socially acceptable; polite society *demands* it. Just type "Silence is Violence" into Google to see what I mean. I thought up the term "criminal (in)justice" to highlight some of the criminal justice system's most common and visible failures brought about by misguided leniency as opposed to punitiveness. So many of the tragic stories whose arcs mirror that of Brittany Hill's killing implicate decisions—made by various criminal justice actors (from lawmakers and prosecutors to judges and police executives)—that resulted in the freedom of someone who could, and should, have been behind bars.

At the root of many of those decisions is a narrative—one that dominates the public discourse—about the nature of criminal justice in the United States of America. That narrative essentially boils down to an assertion that the United States can aptly be described as an oppressive carceral state that has expelled justice from every corner and crevice of its law enforcement apparatus. More specifically, the US is said to be in the midst of an "over" or "mass" incarceration crisis driven by unjustifiably aggressive overpolicing, unduly "coercive" overprosecution, and racism directed primarily at Black and Latino people living in the poorer, "underserved" neighborhoods in and around America's cities.

Such criticisms have been leveled at this country's criminal justice system for at least half a century. But after 2020's violent protests—sparked by the deaths of now household names like George Floyd, Breonna Taylor, and Rayshard Brooks—a growing chorus of professional advocates forcefully pushed this dangerously false narrative further and further into the mainstream. To the extent the assertions highlighted above weren't already regarded as conventional wisdom, they certainly got there by the end of that summer. This put us on the cusp of a generational shift in how our society approaches the core government duty of securing the public against criminal violence, theft, and disorder.

The conventional wisdom, however, reflects conclusions based on fundamental misapprehensions of reality.

From police use of force and "stop-question-and-frisk" to bail and sentencing reform, so much of what we hear from those in favor of depolicing and decarceration is wrong—wrong about both what the relevant data say and the true nature of the issues underlying many of the policy questions being debated in legislatures, classrooms, and cable news studios.

The stakes of these debates are such that these errors are (as the story this book opens with plainly illustrates) rarely harmless. What makes matters worse is that those harms are not evenly distributed throughout the country. The vast majority of America's residents live in peaceful communities that rarely see more than one homicide in a given year, if any. To the extent that there are costs associated with the push to drastically cut back on policing and incarceration (and, as this book will forcefully argue, there are), they're borne disproportionately by the relative handful of communities—often with largely low-income, minority populations—already struggling with elevated levels of crime, disorder, and other social problems. In other words, the same people those pushing for decarceration and depolicing say they're fighting for.

As those costs mount, those who can afford to will escape, leaving those who can't to shoulder the physical, psychological, and economic burdens rising violence imposes on vulnerable communities. This is something I know a bit about, as I am the beneficiary of my parents' decision to escape from 1990s Brooklyn to a Long Island suburb.

AS GROWN UP AS I felt at nine, whenever my parents let me walk to school, the corner store, or Prospect Park with friends, I'd have been lying through my teeth if I denied sometimes feeling afraid—even in the little slice of Brooklyn I called home. But it wasn't the New York Police Department (NYPD) or endemic racism that made me anxious. In the 1990s, getting mugged or beaten up in my own neighborhood always felt like more than a remote possibility. That sense of wariness was dull and could easily be forgotten if I was distracted. But it was always there, just under the surface.

That anxiety disappeared when we moved to a mostly white town in suburban Long Island. At school, no one looked like me. And as a half Dominican, half Puerto Rican kid with, uh, different hair, "the new kid from *Brooklyn*" got teased a bit—even racially taunted, on occasion. It was a heartbreaking transition in 1996: I hadn't wanted to leave our two-bedroom apartment on Ocean Parkway, between Church and Caton. I didn't care that my sister and I would have our own rooms and even a swimming pool in the backyard. And as much as I loved baseball, I was unmoved by the fact that Nassau County's Little League fields were in far better condition than the Parade Ground's fields near Prospect Park.

While I wasn't thrilled about my new life in the burbs, I quickly learned that I could ride my brand-new chrome GT Dyno without even the slightest hint of fear that someone might snatch it out from under me. Eventually, I grew to both understand and appreciate the decision my parents made to move my sister and me out to what they felt would be a safer, more nurturing environment. I also grew to realize that I was a fortunate beneficiary of an incredible privilege: Being born to parents that, albeit by the skin of their teeth, could *afford* to leave a high-crime city for a low-crime suburb meant that I could live my most formative years in a place where violent crime just wasn't something people worried about.

Decades later, I would make the same decision for my son: In the months before he was born, my wife and I often found ourselves discussing the quality of life in our slowly gentrifying East Harlem neighborhood, which at the time was getting harder and harder to imagine pushing a baby stroller through. So we decided to move farther away from our workplaces to the safer, cleaner neighborhood of Forest Hills, where our family was far less likely to encounter the sort of crime and disorder we'd seen in East Harlem.

Though things in Harlem weren't anywhere close to as bad as they were in mid-1990s Brooklyn, I found myself thinking again about my family's move to Long Island and the reasons behind it. I also found myself thinking about how many families living in neighborhoods far more dangerous than the one I moved away from have no choice but to stick it out. Whatever that number was, it was too high, which in many ways is the impetus for this book.

FROM AT LEAST THE time that the late Howard Cosell declared to a horrified national TV audience during the 1977 World Series that "The Bronx is burning,"[3] New York City had been known as the epicenter of a national crime epidemic. Thirteen years later, the city's murder total would peak with more than 2,200 lives lost in 1990.[4]

But by 1996, a look at the top-line statistics would have supported *some* cautious optimism. And even during the peak years, the violence in the neighborhood I called home (within the confines of the 66th Precinct) wasn't what it was in the nearby 70th, 71st, or 67th Precincts, whose borders ranged from a few short blocks to a little over a mile away from our building. Thanks in significant (though not exclusive) part to the police department's successful integration of "broken windows"—a theory posited by the late George L. Kelling and James Q. Wilson in their famous *Atlantic Monthly* article by the same title[5]—into its policing strategy under William "Bill" Bratton, New York was, by 1996, in the early stages of what would turn out to be a historic decline in crime. But our proximity to some of Brooklyn's worst neighborhoods (and a shooting on our block earlier that year) was enough to sustain a real fear of crime despite the progress.

According to my parents, one of their biggest worries was that, despite their best attempts to raise me the right way, I'd fall in with the wrong crowd and become a source of the fears they and so many others felt at the time.

The average Brooklyn resident's sense of security just wasn't very high in the mid-1990s. This was understandable, as Kelling explained in a 1998 article coauthored with Bratton in the *Journal of Law and Criminology:* It wasn't until "after 1995 or 1996" that the impact of the gargantuan police effort led by Bratton "started to be felt."[6]

One couldn't expect the psychological conditioning New Yorkers had undergone over the previous decade to be undone in a snap. It would take years for people to incorporate what the statistics were showing in 1996 into how they went about their daily lives. My parents and I were no exception, particularly since our perceptions were largely informed (and perhaps even skewed) by what my father—then in his fifth year as an NYPD detective assigned to Brooklyn's Robbery Squad—had been witnessing on a daily basis since he joined the department in 1983.

His experiences on the job were, in many ways, an extension of the mess he had grown up in while being raised by a single mom in the (now highly desirable) neighborhood he always derisively yet affectionately referred to as "Park Slop—I mean—Slope."

THIS BOOK ISN'T GOING to fit itself neatly beside those parroting the dominant narratives about criminal justice in America; it's going to push back. If there's one thing you should understand, it's that the arguments that follow proceed from a deeply held belief that the most important disparity we need to address in the United States is the difference between the violent crime rates of our nation's most dangerous and safest neighborhoods.

That concern runs up against the narratives pushed by those pursuing reform—not just from the fringes, but also from within mainstream institutions.

Some examples: In 2017, Senators Chris Coons and Thom Tillis wrote for CNN.com that "America's criminal justice system is broken, focusing far too much on criminalization and incarceration and far too little on rehabilitation."[7] In a *New York Times* article pushing police abolition, a self-described "organizer against criminalization" argued that "The only way to diminish police violence is to reduce contact between the public and the police."[8] And in the *New York Times Magazine*, one writer asserted in 2019 that our criminal justice system is defined by "a fear of Black people and a taste for violent crime."[9]

What's remarkable about so many of the arguments that will be addressed in this book is the degree to which they mirror those advanced by left-of-center public intellectuals in the latter half of the twentieth century. In his seminal work, *Thinking about Crime*—first published in 1975 and updated in 1983—James Q. Wilson pushed back on the conventional wisdom that informed so much of America's approach to criminal justice policy. He showed empirically that crime control was possible to achieve without fixing the underlying social problems so often identified as its causes. The work that undergirded and flowed from that book informed so much of my thinking on these issues and, by extension, much of what's to come.

As important and lasting as Wilson's impact on the world of public policy has been, many of those leading the national debates about crime, policing, and justice seem to have either forgotten or chosen to ignore the lessons of that work, which have inspired an enormous amount of scholarship, much of which I have spent the last several years consuming and applying in my own effort to push back on the conventional wisdom.

ONE OF THE MOST frustrating aspects of America's necessary and important criminal justice reform debate is the cavalier attitude with which (usually, though not always) well-off advocates living in posh suburban enclaves or luxury city high-rises push policies whose downside risks will be borne by a tiny slice of our most vulnerable citizens living in places most of those advocates wouldn't dare walk through by themselves on a summer night.

The reality is that most criminal justice policy shifts—even relatively radical ones—won't make much of an impact in large swaths of America. Why? Because some places just aren't as vulnerable to crime increases as others. Indeed, an entire subfield of criminology is dedicated to exploring how the physical environment of not just a neighborhood but sometimes even a single street segment can be incredibly conducive to crime in ways that an intersection just two blocks over is not.[10]

When we evaluate criminal justice policy proposals like the mass decarceration programs I'll address in this book, we should do so with that disparity in mind. That is, we must evaluate them with the understanding that while emptying prisons and cutting back on policing may not change a whole lot in neighborhoods like DC's Georgetown, New York's Scarsdale, or California's Beverly Hills, they could wreak havoc in Brooklyn's Brownsville, Chicago's Austin, or Baltimore's Belair-Edison neighborhoods. Yet the troubling disparities illustrated by the incredibly unequal distribution of violent crime in America are largely deflected by activists and the media.

In fact, those who do call for more attention to be given to the violence in America's most dangerous neighborhoods in cities like Detroit, Chicago, Baltimore, New Orleans, Philadelphia, and St. Louis are often chastised for doing so. We're often accused of fear-mongering and distracting from the fact that *nationally* crime is quite low, relative to modern peaks.[11]

But using national crime rates to suggest a general direction *the nation* ought to take as to criminal justice questions is exactly the wrong way to approach these issues. The limited utility of national crime rates stems from the fact that they aggregate crime data. Why is this a problem? Because we don't live in the aggregate. So the crime rate of a large geographical area like a country, state, or city tells us essentially zero about what life is like in a particular place at a particular time.

Were you to be randomly dropped over a point in the United States, the chances are pretty good that you'd land somewhere with a murder rate close to zero. Were this exercise to be repeated with, say, 10,000 others, an unlucky few will find themselves in neighborhoods with homicide rates that approach those in some of the most dangerous places on earth.

Unfortunately, the advocates obfuscate this important reality, among others.

Such obfuscation is evidenced by the widespread though misguided belief that the United States suffers from an overincarceration problem. This is not to say that there isn't a subset of the country's prison and jail populations whose incarceration does not serve a legitimate penological end. But the vast majority of American prisoners are violent, chronic offenders. As such, a drastic reduction in the incarcerated population would put many of those living in our country's most vulnerable neighborhoods at risk—as would a sharp curtailment of the proactive policing practices that helped drive the great crime decline of the 1990s. Such a curtailment is another dangerous policy idea to pursue, and like mass decarceration, it is the product of a misapprehension of reality. According to advocates of depolicing, violence is endemic to American law enforcement. Therefore, they argue, we must reduce its footprint. But they're wrong.

It's important to recognize that the criminal justice system is not perfect and that there *is* room for improvement. Some of that improvement falls into the category of making the system less harsh. But if the most important goal is to improve the quality of life in America's most dangerous neighborhoods, the pursuit of that goal must reflect a recognition of the reality that our criminal justice system sometimes—indeed often—fails to be harsh enough.

THE ONGOING DEBATES OVER the questions raised by America's criminal justice reform movement have the potential to transform our society for a generation. Getting those questions wrong (in either direction) will have destructive effects. The aim of this book is to ground these debates in data and the sometimes harsh realities they reflect, because to sidestep those realities is to sacrifice the safety and welfare of our most vulnerable citizens on the altar of political expediency and performative virtue. In other words, this book aims to illustrate that, whether we're talking about incarceration, policing, or prosecution, the harshest and loudest condemnations of the country's criminal justice system are often shallow (that is, lacking nuance) and/or at odds with the available data. Succeeding on that front will, I hope, encourage a more balanced approach to criminal justice reform—one that prioritizes crime control and its attendant benefits.

# CHAPTER ONE

# CONTEXTUALIZING THE REFORM DEBATE

One way to think about this book is as a contribution to ongoing debates about the wisdom of and necessity for mass decarceration and depolicing—debates that became considerably more intense during the tumultuous year of 2020. After all, I hadn't seriously considered writing a book on this subject until I saw jurisdictions from coast to coast responding to the public critiques that followed the murder of George Floyd by rapidly accelerating the implementation of a policy agenda that, to my mind, could most kindly be characterized as a set of experiments, or a series of sizeable bets against the odds.

In state after state and city after city, policymakers were pursuing, among other things, drastic cuts to pretrial and post-conviction incarceration, reductions in the budgets of police departments, the decriminalization of public order offenses, and new limits on police enforcement. In order to make the case for this approach, we saw more and more elected officials, media figures, and activists viciously demonize the institutions that played central roles in the public safety gains made across the country through the last decade of the twentieth century. To these self-styled "reformers," mass decarceration and depolicing were public policy goods unto themselves. But from where I was sitting, it seemed like there was a pretty good chance their approach would create the conditions for an erosion of public safety whose impact would be disproportionately felt by the very communities in whose names these policy experiments were being conducted.

The road toward decarceration and depolicing was not one started down in 2020. It's one that different jurisdictions have been on and off since at least the 1960s. In his 2016 book, *The Rise and Fall of Violent Crime in America*, criminologist Barry Latzer quoted crime historian Eric Monkkonen, who suggested decades ago that criminal violence would follow a cyclical pattern: "[R]ising violence provokes a multitude of control efforts," he said. But when "the murder rate ebbs, control efforts get relaxed, thus creating the multiple conditions causing the next upswing."[1]

Beginning in the late 1970s, some parts of the country began to get tougher on crime in response to upticks in violence and riots that some cities began to see in the late 1960s. That hardening of the criminal justice system really picked up in the mid-1980s through the mid-1990s with the proliferation of mandatory minimum sentences for certain offenses, three-strikes laws, truth-in-sentencing regimes, and new investments (and advancements) in proactive policing.

By the late 1990s, as violent crime rates began to decline sharply, calls to take our foot off the gas became more politically palatable. Those calls had of course predated the 1990s, but the growing crime problems plaguing cities in the 1970s and 1980s seemed to have the effect of suppressing their popularity. Those calls grew louder through the first decade of the 2000s, and support for the idea that we had overcorrected in the punitive direction gained more steam in academic and policy circles. Around 2010, if not earlier, concern about the excesses of policing and the criminal justice system more broadly seemed to reach a critical mass as years of violent crime declines made the 1990s seem so far away, which drove new efforts to address allegations of overpolicing and "mass incarceration." The reformers were attacking on all fronts.

Class action lawsuits were filed against police departments (like the NYPD) to attack practices like stop, question, and frisk.[2] Similar suits were filed against correctional systems as a way to reduce incarceration—as was done in the state of California, whose legislature enacted the Public Safety Realignment Act of 2011[3] to comply with a court order related to litigation wherein the plaintiffs successfully argued that overcrowding in California state prisons created unconstitutionally cruel conditions.[4] In addition to lawsuits, sentencing reform efforts of all sorts were having success across the country. In 2009, per the left-leaning Vera Institute of Justice, New York "essentially dismantled" the Rockefeller Drug Laws (which established mandatory minimums in the 1970s for certain drug offenses).[5] And in 2010, Congress passed and President Barack Obama signed into law the Fair Sentencing Act, which eliminated the sentencing disparity between crack and powder cocaine violations.[6]

Many of these efforts—which are just a few examples of what was a growing trend—were backed by influential activists and academics who did their part to advance the cause in the public square. One prominent example of this was Michelle Alexander's 2010 bestselling book, *The New Jim Crow: Mass Incarceration in the Age of Colorblindness*, in which she argued that drug enforcement was driving Black men into prisons, where they were disenfranchised and exploited in ways akin to what was done to Black Americans in the South through the mid-twentieth century.

By 2010 it was beginning to seem as though there just wasn't any room (or tolerance) for the idea that policing and incarceration were legitimate societal enterprises. Things took an even more radical turn in the years that followed, and viral police use of force incidents were a major reason for this.

Controversial police uses of force were certainly nothing new in the United States. I remember my parents talking about and watching the news coverage of the beating of Rodney King by police officers in Los Angeles back when I was in grade school in 1991. What was different about the 2010s was twofold.

First, there was a large (and fast-growing) segment of the population that was spending more and more time on social media platforms like Facebook and Twitter, which allowed for the instantaneous dissemination of information (and misinformation) and amplified incidents that might not have captured as much attention in a different era. An example of this was how quickly the apparently false claim that Michael Brown had his hands up in surrender when he was shot by former police officer Darren Wilson in Ferguson, Missouri, in 2014 became a rallying cry. Chants of "Hands up, don't shoot!" could be heard throughout the crowds that rioted in the streets following the shooting, and the phrase is still chanted during protests of police actions today.

Second, by the 2010s, a huge portion of the population was equipped with cell phone cameras, which meant there was a much higher chance of police uses of force being filmed and widely disseminated by bystanders, who were essentially transformed into citizen journalists. This, I think, had the effect of contributing to the increasingly widespread sense that police uses of force were far more common than they actually were. It also had the effect of driving more visceral reactions to force incidents as more people actually got to see these things take place. Two examples that come to mind are the cell phone videos of what seemed to be Philando Castile's final breaths after he was shot by a police officer in Minnesota, and of Eric Garner repeating the phrase "I can't breathe" during his arrest by NYPD officers, after which he went into cardiac arrest and died. It would be hard for anyone to watch those videos and not be disturbed by the sounds of men gasping for what would turn out to be their final breaths—and in the case of Castile, to watch a man die in front of a four-year-old child, who will have to deal with the trauma of having witnessed something even battle-hardened soldiers struggle to live with.

These events gave the push for reform an intense new boost, impacting both legislative agendas and political outcomes—particularly in local prosecutor races. Indeed, after 2014, the so-called progressive prosecutor movement took off as self-styled reformers—some of whom were former public defenders and civil rights litigators—vied to head up district, county, and state's attorney offices, promising to cut incarceration and prosecute police violence. Many of them emerged victorious in major metro areas across the country, like St. Louis, Houston, Orlando, Chicago, Boston, Dallas, Philadelphia, Northern Virginia, Baltimore, Brooklyn, Portland, Austin, San Francisco, Los Angeles, and Manhattan.

In the lead-up to 2020, much of the broader public had already been primed to believe that police were an out-of-control occupying force, and that their violence was being aided and abetted by a justice system built and operated (by design, according to some) to the specific detriment of Black and brown communities. ("Black and brown" reflect two more colloquialisms that aren't technically correct, but that I'll risk using so as not to distract from the book's more central points.)

Helping things along were media figures like Ava DuVernay, who produced, directed, and wrote the Oscar-nominated and Emmy Award–winning 2016 documentary *13th*, which took the case advanced by Michelle Alexander, who was also featured in the film, to an even larger audience. DuVernay also produced, directed, and wrote the Peabody– and Emmy Award–winning 2019 Netflix miniseries *When They See Us*, which offered a harsh critique of the criminal justice system through a compelling, if contested,[7] telling of the story of the "Central Park Five."

Even before 2020, in the popular media and academia, skepticism toward the harshest critiques of policing and criminal justice were being met with the recitations of the now household names invoked as proof of the justice system's racist failings: Trayvon Martin, Michael Brown, Eric Garner, Stephon Clark, Philando Castile, Laquan McDonald, Walter Scott, Sandra Bland, Kalief Browder, Tamir Rice, Freddie Gray . . . At this point, efforts to reform policing and criminal justice were enjoying ever more forward momentum. But the 2020 deaths of Ahmaud Arbery, Breonna Taylor, George Floyd, and Rayshard Brooks seemed to break the proverbial camel's back, violently shoving the reform movement into overdrive. What followed was a wave of anti-police sentiment, a subsequent pullback on the part of police, and a slew of far-reaching policy shifts that—like many (though not all) of those instituted during the preceding decade—sharply raised the transaction costs of law enforcement while lowering the transaction costs of lawbreaking.

What followed that was the single-largest annual spike in homicides in American history.

For the first time since the mid-1990s, the United States saw more than 21,000 murders in 2020, a 30 percent increase over 2019, which is the biggest year-over-year increase on record.

The year 2020 was preceded by a decade-long trend of

- Increasingly vitriolic expressions of anti-police rhetoric in the media and academia.

- Decarceration (between 2009 and 2019, the country's imprisonment rate declined 17 percent).[8]

- Depolicing (during the same period, arrests declined by more than 25 percent, going from more than 13.6 million[9] to just over 10 million,[10] while the number of full-time police officers working American cities went from about 452,000 in 2009[11] down to 443,000 in 2019).[12]

Each of these trends accelerated for various reasons in 2020.[13]

Rather than consider the possibility that decarceration and depolicing may have contributed to the crime spike, some in the reformer camp have argued that the pandemic's impact on the economy was to blame. Representative Alexandria Ocasio-Cortez, a Democrat from New York, for example, named pandemic-driven "record unemployment" and "economic desperation" as potential causes of what would turn out to be the city's largest-ever single-year spike in homicides since at least the 1960s.[14] Undercutting the congresswoman's suggestion were the facts that (1) despite the global nature of the pandemic, many other similarly impacted nations (like Canada, the United Kingdom, France, Germany, and Mexico) did not see their homicides spike, and (2) despite the nationwide impact of the pandemic here in the US, violence seemed to remain as geographically and demographically concentrated as ever.

Now, this is not a book about the causes of the spike in serious violent crime that began in 2020 and continued through 2021. Nevertheless, it's worth elaborating on two points I think will help readers better understand the anti-decarceration/depolicing cases made in the forthcoming chapters:

1. As was illustrated by the unequal distribution of the additional shootings and homicides in 2020, serious violent crime is (and has long been) hyper-concentrated in the United States—both geographically (in small slices of metro areas) and demographically (among young, disproportionately Black and Latino males). As such, the social costs of crime have never been evenly distributed. This is important insofar as it illustrates just who stands to pay the price for policy initiatives that hurt public safety.

2. The attribution of America's homicide spike to the economic impact of the global novel coronavirus pandemic implies a relationship between criminal violence and socioeconomic indicators like poverty and unemployment that the available data simply don't support.

## A NOTE ON CRIME CONCENTRATION

If you board an uptown express train at Grand Central Terminal, you can be in the heart of Manhattan's Upper East Side, on 86th Street and Lexington Avenue, in just two stops. There, you'll be just steps away from some of New York's most prized real estate, its finest museums, and coffee shops slinging five-dollar lattes expertly crafted by pink-haired baristas. But if you stay on that express train for just a few more minutes—just one more stop a mere two miles up the avenue—you'll step out onto the platform of a station with a very different feel (and smell). What you'll see in the area of 125th Street and Lexington Avenue is a much less hopeful and much more dangerous scene: open-air drug dealing and intoxicated men passed out on sidewalks coated with urine and feces (among other things). In 2020, the precinct that covers the first of these two subway stops saw one shooting and one homicide, while the one that covers the latter saw 20 shootings and 10 homicides.[15] In New York City—indeed, in most cities— things can change that quickly.

Sometimes, you'll hear people talk about a city's, county's, state's, or country's violent crime problem. It's an understandable colloquialism, but it's not technically right. This is because crime is so hyper-concentrated that one's risk of victimization can sometimes shift dramatically by simply walking a couple of blocks in either direction.

As I mentioned in the introduction, if you were to randomly drop 10,000 people over the United States, the overwhelming majority of them will land someplace with a murder rate close to zero. An unlucky few, however, will drop into neighborhoods with homicide rates rivaling those of some of the most dangerous places in the world.

According to a county-level analysis done by the Crime Prevention Research Center, just 2 percent of US counties (home to just 28 percent of the population as of 2014) see about 50 percent of US murders in a given year.[16] More than half (54 percent) of US counties don't see any murders in a given year. Within those counties, criminal homicides—as well as violent and property crimes more generally—are concentrated within urban enclaves.[17] The practical implication of this is that people who reside in the same city can live with widely disparate risks of criminal victimization. Chicago—my wife's hometown, and a city I called home for three years—is illustrative of this point.

## AN ILLUSTRATIVE BREAKDOWN

In 2019, there were 16,425 incidents of murder and non-negligent manslaughter in the United States. With a population of 328,239,523, that meant a national murder rate of 5.0 per 100,000.[18] Illinois—home to 3.9 percent (12,723,071) of the country's population—saw 832 (5.1 percent) of the country's murders, giving the state a higher 2019 murder rate of 6.5 per 100,000.[19] Chicago saw 492 (nearly 60 percent) of the state's homicides, despite housing just 21.3 percent (2,707,064) of the state's population.[20] This gave Chicago a significantly higher murder rate of 18.2 per 100,000. But if you were to single out the 10 community areas with the highest murder tallies that year (home to just 15.6 percent of the city's population), you'd see 53 percent of the cities' killings, which gets you an even more staggering collective homicide rate of 61.7 per 100,000—more than triple the citywide rate and more than 12 times the national rate.

In these 10 community areas, where between 90 percent and 98 percent of the residents are either Black or Hispanic/Latino, the homicide rates in 2019 ranged from a low of 40.8 per 100,000 to a high of 131.9 per 100,000 (see table 1). To put it another way, these 10 neighborhoods saw 12 times more murders than they would have if killings were evenly distributed across the population.

## TABLE 1

| Community Area | 2019 Murders* | Estimated Population† | 2019 Murder Rate (per 100K)‡ | % Black & Hispanic/Latino† |
|---|---|---|---|---|
| Auburn Gresham | 20 | 44,878 | 44.6 | 97.6% |
| Austin | 53 | 96,557 | 51.7 | 92.9% |
| Englewood | 19 | 24,369 | 78.0 | 98.3% |
| Greater Grand Crossing | 26 | 31,471 | 82.6 | 97.4% |
| Humboldt Park | 28 | 54,165 | 51.7 | 90.4% |
| North Lawndale | 23 | 34,794 | 66.1 | 95.0% |
| Roseland | 27 | 38,816 | 69.6 | 96.4% |
| South Shore | 22 | 53,971 | 40.8 | 95.8% |
| West Englewood | 20 | 26,647 | 75.1 | 97.1% |
| West Garfield Park | 23 | 17,433 | 131.9 | 96.1% |
| **TOTAL** | **261** | **423,101** | **61.7** | **95.7% (Avg.)** |

\* Murder tallies are taken from the Chicago Police Department's 2019 Annual Report (https://home.chicagopolice.org/wp-content/uploads/2020/09/19AR.pdf).
† Population data were taken from the Chicago Metropolitan Agency for Planning's Community Data Snapshots on November 21, 2021, which includes estimates from the 2020 census (https://www.cmap.illinois.gov/data/community-snapshots).
‡ Murder rates are rounded up to the nearest tenth.

Compare those 10 community areas with the 28 that saw one or fewer homicides that year (home to 25.4 percent of the city's population), and you'd get a much safer picture—250 fewer murders (just 2.2 percent of the city's total) despite housing 263,985 *more* residents, getting you a collective homicide rate of 1.6 per 100,000 (see table 2).

## TABLE 2

| Community Area | 2019 Murders* | Estimated Population† | 2019 Murder Rate (per 100K)‡ | % Black & Hispanic/Latino† |
|---|---|---|---|---|
| Albany Park | 1 | 48,396 | 2.1 | 49.9% |
| Archer Heights | 0 | 14,196 | 0.0 | 78.4% |
| Beverly | 0 | 20,027 | 0.0 | 39.1% |
| Bridgeport | 0 | 33,702 | 0.0 | 24.9% |
| Burnside | 0 | 2,527 | 0.0 | 98.2% |
| Calumet Heights | 1 | 13,088 | 7.6 | 97.8% |
| Clearing | 1 | 24,473 | 4.1 | 56.4% |
| Edgewater | 0 | 56,296 | 0.0 | 27.3% |
| Edison Park | 1 | 11,525 | 8.7 | 10.5% |
| Forest Glen | 0 | 19,596 | 0.0 | 16.3% |
| Hegewisch | 0 | 10,027 | 0.0 | 64.7% |
| Hermosa | 0 | 24,062 | 0.0 | 86.4% |
| Hyde Park | 0 | 29,456 | 0.0 | 33.8% |
| Jefferson Park | 0 | 26,216 | 0.0 | 25.8% |
| Kenwood | 1 | 19,116 | 5.2 | 69.8% |
| Lincoln Square | 0 | 40,494 | 0.0 | 21.6% |
| McKinley Park | 1 | 15,923 | 6.3 | 57.8% |
| Montclare | 0 | 14,401 | 0.0 | 62.6% |
| Mount Greenwood | 0 | 18,628 | 0.0 | 14.0% |
| Near South Side | 1 | 28,795 | 3.5 | 29.4% |
| North Center | 1 | 35,114 | 2.8 | 13.6% |
| North Park | 0 | 17,559 | 0.0 | 22.9% |
| Norwood Park | 0 | 38,303 | 0.0 | 15.9% |
| Oakland | 1 | 6,799 | 14.7 | 95.2% |
| O'Hare | 0 | 13,418 | 0.0 | 12.6% |
| South Deering | 1 | 14,105 | 7.1 | 95.9% |
| West Lawn | 1 | 33,662 | 3.0 | 86.7% |
| Uptown | 0 | 57,182 | 0.0 | 32.4% |
| **TOTAL** | **11** | **687,086** | **1.6** | **47.9% (Avg.)** |

* Murder tallies are taken from the Chicago Police Department's 2019 Annual Report (https://home.chicagopolice.org/wp-content/uploads/2020/09/19AR.pdf).
† Population data were taken from the Chicago Metropolitan Agency for Planning's Community Data Snapshots on November 21, 2021, which includes estimates from the 2020 census (https://www.cmap.illinois.gov/data/community-snapshots).
‡ Murder rates are rounded up to the nearest tenth.

**I MOVED TO CHICAGO** to attend law school back in 2012. My wife and I lived in a beautiful building on a quiet block in the northern tip of Lakeview, just off of Lake Shore Drive. Our building had a gym, a well-manicured courtyard, and a 24-hour concierge. The neighborhood was nice. Scenic bike paths, coffee shops, and restaurants were all within walking distance, as was the famed home of the Chicago Cubs, Wrigley Field. In our little slice of the city's 19th police district, crime really wasn't a daily concern when we left the house. It was a different story near the southern border of the city's 25th police district—just north of the 15th (consistently one of the city's most dangerous)—where my in-laws live. In 2020, the 19th District saw just 4 homicides and 19 non-fatal shootings, while the 25th saw 20 homicides and 113 non-fatal shootings (many of which were concentrated near the border of the 15th District, which saw 64 homicides in 2020).

Our Chicago experience was, to put it mildly, quite different from those who were not fortunate enough to live in the city's safer enclaves. But even in the relatively little amount of time we spent on the West Side, my wife and I experienced firsthand just how dangerous things could get.

A few weeks before we moved back to New York in the summer of 2015, my wife and I had spent the day with my mother-in-law. We dropped her off at home in the late afternoon and were making our way east toward the lake. As we waited to turn onto Central Avenue from Fullerton, I noticed the driver of the car stopped at the same light on the opposite side of the road exit his vehicle. Another car was speeding past the left side of ours from behind, on the wrong side of the double yellow line. As that car made the left turn we were waiting to make, the man who had exited his car began shooting at it. After a few pulls of the trigger, he got back into his vehicle and gave chase.

Those bullets came within feet of us. It all happened so fast that I don't think I fully processed what happened until long after the shooting had stopped. We pulled over, called the cops, gave our statement, and went home. We never heard back from the police. We left for New York later that summer, but our worries came with us. After all, our family still lives in that neighborhood.

The concentration of crime has been getting more attention in recent years thanks to the work of criminologist David Weisburd. Weisburd's analyses have established what he calls "the law of crime concentration," which, in his words, states that "for a defined measure of crime at a specific micro-geographic unit, the concentration of crime will fall within a narrow bandwidth of percentages for a defined cumulative proportion of crime."[21] What does that mean in more practical terms? Well, according to several analyses of cities of varying sizes, Weisburd and his colleagues have found that somewhere in the range of 4 percent of a city's street segments[22] will see somewhere in the range of 50 percent of that city's total crime, and about 1.5 percent of a city's street segments will see about 25 percent of that city's crime.[23]

In a study of crime concentration in New York City, Weisburd and his colleague Taryn Zastrow found that in 2010, 2015, and 2020, between 3.7 and 4.2 percent of the city's street segments saw 50 percent of all violent crimes in those years.[24] Between 1.01 and 1.12 percent of Big Apple street segments saw 25 percent of violent crimes in those years.[25]

Violent crimes like homicide aren't just geographically concentrated. They're also demographically concentrated. In

New York, since at least 2008, a minimum of 95 percent of the city's shooting victims have been either Black or Hispanic.[26] Nationally, while Black people constitute 13.4 percent of the population,[27] they made up more than 53 percent of the nation's homicide victims in 2020 (see figure 1). That disparity becomes even starker once you consider that the vast majority of homicide victims are male.

Black US residents have accounted for an outsized share of America's homicides for decades. But Black people also bore the brunt of 2020's homicide spike. While the share of homicide victims constituted by white people declined by 2.4 percentage points in 2020 relative to 2019, the share constituted by Black and Hispanic people increased by 2.2 percentage points (see figure 1).

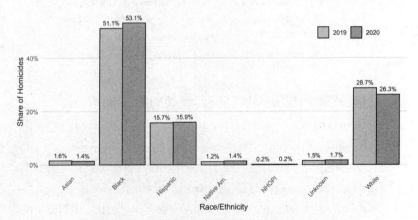

**Figure 1. Share of Homicides by Race/Ethnicity and Year**
*Source: FBI Supplemental Homicide Report/Jacob Kaplan*

And while Black people already had the highest homicide victimization rate (19.5 per 100,000) of any group in 2019, the disparity grew even starker in 2020, when that number shot up to 25.3 per 100,000—almost *10 times* the white rate of 2.6 per 100,000 (see figure 2).

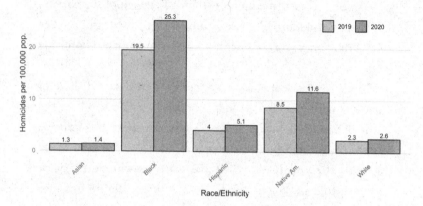

**Figure 2. Homicide Rates by Race/Ethnicity and Year**
*Source: FBI Supplemental Homicide Report/Jacob Kaplan. Population estimates from 2019 ACS/IPUMS, Census Bureau estimate of monthly postcensal resident population vintage July 2020.*

## THE OVERSTATED IMPORTANCE OF SOCIOECONOMIC (AND OTHER) "ROOT CAUSES"

In the summer of 2015, Thaddeus "T.J." Jimenez wasn't poor. In fact, he was a millionaire—many times over. He drove an expensive Mercedes convertible sports car and wore gold chains around his neck. After winning a $25 million settlement in 2012 in a wrongful conviction lawsuit, Jimenez could have gone anywhere in the world to lead one of the many lives his newfound wealth would have sustained. Instead, he went back to his West Side Chicago neighborhood and doubled down on the gangbanger lifestyle.

In August 2015, he and an associate livestreamed themselves driving around a West Side Chicago neighborhood with a police scanner in tow to make sure they weren't being observed.[28] They were armed with pistols and what some might call an "assault" rifle as they "r[ode] around looking for flakes," declaring to the camera that "[W]e are the police over here . . . We are the government." Before too long, they found their target—a man who was just getting out of his car. "Why shouldn't I blast you right now?" Jimenez asked the man. Apparently, the target's answer was unsatisfactory, because what followed were two gunshots fired at close range. So far as I can tell, the victim was not robbed, and there was no indication that he owed Jimenez a cent—let alone an amount large enough to matter to someone recently graced with an eight-figure windfall. Nor did this shooting of an unarmed man improve Jimenez's financial prospects; he was quickly arrested and charged, which surely cost him.

If you're wondering why this man would waste a well-financed second chance "rebuilding his old gang," as the *Chicago Tribune* put it in a story following the shooting,[29] you won't find an answer in the socioeconomic indicators many people think of as drivers of violent crime. After all, Jimenez was loaded (no pun intended).

FOR MUCH OF THE twentieth century, we were told that the idea that improving socioeconomic indicators like poverty rates through more government spending, minimum wage hikes, and the like was a necessary step on the road to less urban crime—which, we were told, was an artifact of poverty, inequality, and underinvestment. However, a handful of skeptical scholars, like James Q.

Wilson and George L. Kelling, rejected this idea and laid the groundwork for a nationwide urban crime decline that began in the 1990s and, in some cities, went on for more than two decades. That decline came even as socioeconomic indicators like urban poverty rates remained essentially steady.

In New York City, for example, between 1990 and 2018, homicides declined from 2,262 to just 295. What happened to the city's poverty rate during that time frame? In 1989, the year before New York's homicides peaked, the poverty rate was 18.8 percent.[30] In 2016, the year before homicides hit their modern low, the poverty rate was slightly *higher* at 19.5 percent.[31]

The city's crime decline continued unabated during the financial crisis that made New York one of the cities hit hardest by the Great Recession of 2007–2009. Between 2006 and 2009 (which captures the financial crisis that caused a deep recession), New York City's unemployment rate for working-age Black men—who constitute most of the city's homicide and shooting victims and perpetrators—nearly doubled, jumping from 9 percent to 17.9 percent.[32] However, the city's homicides fell to 471 in 2009 from 596 in 2006, while felony assaults declined to 16,773 from 17,309.

Nationally, the nation's homicide rate declined 15 percent (dropping from 5.7 per 100,000 to 4.8) between 2007 and 2010, while the nation's unemployment rate nearly doubled during the same period, spiking from 4.6 percent to 9.3 percent. And though income inequality grew in the US by about 20 percent between 1980 and 2016,[33] the country's violent crime rate declined from 593.5 per 100,000 in 1981[34] to 386.3 in 2016.[35]

There is, to put it mildly, a bit of a disconnect between violent crime and socioeconomic indicators like poverty, unemployment, and income inequality. That disconnect has been illustrated by a number of criminologists over the decades. Barry Latzer, for example, does a brilliant job of documenting what he calls "crime/adversity mismatch" in his 2016 book, *The Rise and Fall of Violent Crime in America*, which makes a convincing case that the available data cannot establish a "consistent relationship between the extent of a group's socioeconomic disadvantage and its level of violence." In New York, for example, Black people experience poverty at a lower rate (19.2 percent) than their Hispanic (23.9 percent) and Asian (24.1 percent) counterparts, who account for much smaller shares of the city's gun violence.[36] Latzer makes this point to argue that a culture of violence underlies much of the racial disparity in criminal offending patterns—a thesis that is not without support from the work of other scholars.

Despite incongruity with the data presented above, the idea that crime control depends on reducing economic inequality, addressing unemployment, and alleviating poverty continues to persist. For example, Philadelphia's "progressive" district attorney, Larry Krasner, has consistently blamed that city's rising violence on, among other things, "poverty [and] hopelessness,"[37] and has suggested that the upward trend of shootings and homicides under his tenure is at least partly a function of children not having "regular access to nutritious meals . . . [or] reliable after-school options."[38] Krasner has yet to offer any evidence that there has been a significant enough change in these measures to account for the growth in violence in the city of Philadelphia which broke its all-time homicide record in 2021.

While improving the material well-being of America's disadvantaged Black and brown communities is commonly offered up as a way to cut crime, it's worth noting that Latzer has documented massive improvements in various measures of well-being among Black Americans over the course of the twentieth century. Latzer noted:

- By the end of the 1950s, earnings for Black males reached "250% of their prewar level."[39]

- Between 1940 and 1960, the percentage of dwellings where Black people lived that were owner occupied increased by 65 percent.[40]

- The proportion of Black male household heads in poverty went from 70.8 percent in 1949 down to 21.5 percent in 1969.[41]

Notwithstanding this trend, the age-adjusted male homicide victimization rate for Black people went from 47.0 per 100,000 in 1950 to 78.2 per 100,000 in 1970.[42]

Latzer went on to note that "the percentage of the poverty class continued to decline through the 1970s—to as low as 11 percent by 1973."[43] Yet by the 1970s, the US had seen an enormous increase in violent crime.

The fact is that violent crime has ebbed and flowed in jurisdictions across the country in ways that don't track with the sort of socioeconomic indicators opponents of enforcement-centric approaches to crime often point to as root causes of violence. New York City didn't solve poverty in the 1990s. I've yet to read the socioeconomic root cause story of New York's victory on the violent crime front. What *did* change was how crime and disorder were policed and punished.

While it's true that many of those who enter our criminal justice system for violent offenses are un- or underemployed, un- or undereducated, and financially insecure, there are millions of people in similar circumstances across this country who never shoot, kill, assault, rape, or rob anyone. And they outnumber the criminals by a lot! There are, however, other attributes common to many offenders that can go a long way toward explaining their behavior: deep-seated senses of entitlement, antisocial dispositions, and substance use disorders.

As I noted in a report (forthcoming, as of this writing) I coauthored with criminologists Matthew DeLisi and John Paul Wright, "In laboratory settings, entitlement [defined in the *Diagnostic and Statistical Manual of Mental Disorders* as 'unreasonable expectations of especially favorable treatment or automatic compliance with his or her expectations'] is among the best predictors of various forms of aggression, and is consistent with a highly antagonistic approach toward interpersonal dealings that is positively correlated with odd and eccentric, and dramatic and emotional personality disorders."[44] It's worth noting that one of those disorders, antisocial personality disorder (ASPD), has an estimated prevalence in the general male population of between 2 and 4 percent.[45] Among male prisoners, however, prevalence estimates range between 40 and 70 percent.[46] Poverty (defined in 2021 as an individual income below $12,880[47]), by contrast, is much more prevalent among the general public than ASPD—ranging between 11.8 percent in 2018 and 11.4 percent in 2020[48]—and less prevalent among male prisoners.[49] Our paper went on to note: "[D]rug use is far less prevalent in the general population than it is in correctional settings—even when you exclude those incarcerated primarily for drug-related offenses. Data from the National Survey on Drug Use and Health[50] indicate that 79.2 percent of Americans over the age of twelve have not used an illicit drug in the past year; half [that] population has *never* used an illicit drug."[51]

A Bureau of Justice Statistics report, using data from 2007 to 2009, found that 58 percent of state prisoners and 63 percent of sentenced jail inmates met the diagnostic criteria for drug abuse or dependence.[52]

## CONCLUSION

That the risk of violent victimization can be so drastically different for individuals living just a short drive from one another in the same city is something that is wildly underappreciated in contemporary debates about crime and justice, which is a shame because it couldn't be more relevant to many of the points being debated. Among those points are those based on the racial disparities that appear across various measures of law enforcement outcomes—from searches and arrests to prosecutions and incarcerations. It's certainly true, for example, that Black Americans are overrepresented (given their share of the population) among those searched, arrested, and subjected to force by police. But those statistics are at least partly a function of how police resources are deployed, which, in turn, is largely a function of where crime—particularly violent crime—is concentrated. As you saw above, serious violent crimes are often concentrated in geographic areas with large shares of Black and Hispanic/Latino residents. What that means is that those groups will naturally feature more prominently in police enforcement statistics.

Moreover, it's important to understand that analyses based on broader, more macrogeographic units of measurement may deliver results that obscure how things may have changed in the more discrete areas we should be focusing on. Given the concentration of crime, it's common for one neighborhood to be far more susceptible to a crime increase in response to a shift in policing activity or criminal justice policy than another neighborhood in the same jurisdiction. New York City's stop, question, and frisk (SQF) practices provide a good example of this. After the city dropped its appeal of a federal court's opinion that the NYPD's approach to SQF was unconstitutional, the number of stops reported by NYPD officers declined dramatically. The city's crime numbers, however, continued to decline. Critics seized on these two citywide trends to argue that SQF had been an ineffective crime-fighting tool. But we wouldn't have expected the city's safe neighborhoods to suddenly become dangerous in response to a shift in police activity. A better analysis would have focused on the areas in which crime was most heavily concentrated. Weisburd and his colleagues did just that, finding that SQF had a significant, if modest, deterrent effect on crime.[53]

Taking account of the law of crime concentration is an important first step on the path toward the realization that upending the criminal justice system isn't justifiable in the name of racial equity—particularly if you care about the distribution of safety.

Nor can the "reimagining" of criminal justice in America be justified by proposing it alongside large public expenditures that can't actually get at the real root causes of criminal violence. Try as you might, you simply won't find consistent and strong evidence suggesting that crimes like shootings and homicides can be attributed to economic circumstances. That the "socio-economic root causes" idea continues to animate much of the commentary about crime and justice in America distracts us from what I'm convinced is the (grimmer) reality: What drives criminal violence has a lot more to do with the antisocial dispositions of violent criminals and a street culture that elevates violence as both a legitimate means of dispute resolution and a basis for respect. In other words, violent crime is a social problem we can't simply buy our way out from under. What this means is that, at least for now, traditional crime-fighting tools will have to continue to play a central role if we are to maintain the levels of public safety every one of us deserves.

Incarceration is one of those tools. Policing is another. Unfortunately, however, sharply reducing both has become central to the agenda of many criminal justice reformers, some of whom aim to abolish police, jails, and prisons in their entirety. The chapters that follow will make the case against this program by highlighting what the push for mass decarceration and depolicing gets wrong—and who it will hurt most.

# CHAPTER TWO

# AGAINST MASS DECARCERATION, PART 1: POST-CONVICTION INCARCERATION

I n one of his classic bits, Jerry Seinfeld, the king of observational comedy, told us that the most annoying thing about wanted posters is that they beg the following question: "Why didn't they just hold on to this guy *when they were taking his picture*!?"[1] Obviously, we can't (and shouldn't) have a one-strike-and-you're-out policy whereby anyone who finds themself in handcuffs will remain incarcerated for life. But as you'll learn in this chapter, the most serious violent crimes are disproportionately committed by individuals with lengthy rap sheets and active criminal justice statuses, and many of these individuals could (and probably should) have been incarcerated at the time of the offenses in question. Seinfeld's relatable frustration seems to stem from a perceived failure of the system to avail itself of what is generally understood to be the central benefit of jails and prisons, the primary penological end these institutions serve: Except in rare cases of escape, these institutions spare the general public from the crimes those incarcerated would have otherwise committed if they were out on the street. This is referred to in the criminological literature as incapacitation. This, in my view, is the most important of the four broad justifications for incarceration. The other three are deterrence, rehabilitation, and retribution.

Incapacitation is one of those benefits that's easy for most of us to take for granted—particularly those of us living in safe places—because most of us (thankfully) don't have much interaction with the sort of people that tend to find themselves in American prisons. Those degrees of separation from high-rate criminal offenders can also lead to an underappreciation of the benefits provided by incarceration, which, in turn, can make us vulnerable to emotionally potent critiques of incarceration as a method of crime control.

This dynamic was captured by the late Richard Pryor, another king of comedy, in the early 1980s. Pryor told the story of spending time interacting with prisoners in an Arizona state penitentiary while filming a movie on the premises with his co-star Gene Wilder. He started off by noting that 80 percent of the inmates in the facility were Black, which, he said, naïvely made his heart ache as a fellow Black man attuned to the ongoing struggle for racial equity and civil rights. After six weeks of interacting with the hardened criminals on location, however, Pryor sheepishly admitted to the crowd that he left with a different view: "Thank God we got penitentiaries."[2]

Funny as these stories from Seinfeld and Pryor are, the far too many real-life examples—like the tragic story of Brittany Hill told in this book's introduction—of what happens when we fail to incapacitate serious offenders are not laughing matters.

Unfortunately, however, the idea that the United States has a "mass incarceration" problem has become increasingly popular since the turn of the 21st century—and not just among activists, but also among popular media figures, academics, public intellectuals, and policymakers, particularly (though by no means exclusively) those on the political left.

Support for a mass decarceration effort seemed to become a litmus test for those pursuing the Democratic nomination for the presidency in 2020.* Here are just a few examples from that election's Democratic candidates:

- Shortly before declaring her candidacy, Massachusetts senator Elizabeth Warren falsely told attendees at the We the People Summit that "More people [are] locked up for low-level offenses on marijuana than for all violent crimes in this country."[3]

- While campaigning for the presidency, now vice president Kamala Harris released a criminal justice plan stating that "It is long past time to re-envision public safety by strengthening and supporting our communities and *drastically limiting* the number of people we expose to our criminal justice system."[4] (emphasis added). Chief among the proposals outlined were "End[ing] the 'War on Drugs'" and "Legaliz[ing] Marijuana."

- In an essay proposal to address mass incarceration, Senator Cory Booker bemoaned that "Since 1980 . . . longer, more

---

* For more extensive, book-length arguments made in the service of mass decarceration proposals, consider reading Rachel E. Barkow's *Prisoners of Politics: Breaking the Cycle of Mass Incarceration*, the Brennan Center for Justice's *Ending Mass Incarceration: Ideas from Today's Leaders*, John F. Pfaff's *Locked In: The True Causes of Mass Incarceration and How to Achieve Real Reform*, Glenn Loury's *Race, Incarceration, and American Values*, Jeremy Travis's *Perspectives on Crime and Justice*, Emily Bazelon's *Charged: The New Movement to Transform American Prosecution and End Mass Incarceration*, and Patrick Sharkey's *Uneasy Peace: The Great Crime Decline, the Renewal of City Life, and the Next War on Violence*.

punitive sentences, often for nonviolent crimes . . . have wasted precious resources by locking people up for low-level crimes instead of focusing on rehabilitation."[5]

- When asked at a campaign event, "Do you commit to cutting incarceration by 50%, if elected?" now president Joe Biden offered this response: "The answer's yes."[6]

Earlier, I referred to the popularity of and widespread subscription to the "mass incarceration" critique as unfortunate. That's because the logical extension of that critique is support for a policy program explicitly aimed at dramatically cutting the number of those incarcerated in the US—a program that can fairly be expected to result (as it almost certainly has already) in more high-rate offenders being free to violently victimize members of their communities. This is no small thing, especially because those places will very often be economically disadvantaged urban enclaves with mostly Black and brown populations that can least afford the disastrous effects that high crime levels have on communities—effects that extend beyond mere property damage and other costs borne by victims of serious violence. Indeed, studies have shown that serious criminal violence affects everything from the mental health[7] to the academic performance[8] of those living in the communities impacted by said violence.

As such, it's worth interrogating the "mass incarceration" critique by sincerely considering the question of whether there are too many people incarcerated in the United States. Advocates of far-reaching reforms that would dramatically reduce incarceration rates usually answer this question in the affirmative by making one or more of the following four arguments:

1. That the United States incarcerates at a significantly higher rate than other developed nations around the globe serves as prima facie evidence that we overincarcerate.

2. A large portion of the incarcerated population—which, decarceration advocates say, consists of "low-level," "nonviolent" offenders—simply doesn't pose enough of a threat to the public's safety to justify their incarceration.

3. Even if an uptick in incarceration was justified by the high violent crime levels of the 1980s and early 1990s, that incarceration levels continued to rise during the decline in violent crime that began in the mid-1990s has rendered current incarceration rates unjustifiably high.

4. Whatever the public safety benefits of incarceration are, they don't outweigh the harms of incarceration, which is itself criminogenic (that is, it creates more crime) and disruptive of family life.

My hope is that what follows will highlight the flaws in these ideas and the harms we can expect if they continue to enjoy widespread support.

## OF COURSE THE US INCARCERATES MORE THAN OTHER NATIONS

At the top of her contribution to the aforementioned compendium of essays published by the left-wing Brennan Center for Justice (a think tank based at New York University's law school), then presidential candidate Kamala Harris lamented that "The

United States currently incarcerates more of its citizens than any other nation in the world. The US has five percent of the world's population but nearly 25 percent of its prisoners"[9]—a statistic also noted in Senator Cory Booker's essay in the same publication.[10] In the same compendium, Senator Bernie Sanders began his essay by noting, "The United States imprisons more people than any other country on earth. Year after year, we continue to exceed every nation—including authoritarian governments like China, Russia, North Korea, and Iran—for the highest incarceration rate in the world."[11]

While the juxtaposition of America's incarcerated population with those of other somewhat similarly situated nations may, at first glance, seem rhetorically powerful, the question of whether our nation overincarcerates on a "mass" scale is not one that can be answered via international comparisons. To present America's incarceration rate alongside that of another Western democracy as prima facie evidence of our overincarceration is to engage in an egregious oversimplification. Why? Because these comparisons mask incredibly important differences that, when accounted for, take the wind out of the comparison's rhetorical sails. In other words, this particular line of argument-by-implication elides critical distinctions that go a long way toward explaining why the US incarcerates at a significantly higher volume and rate than, say, Germany, England, and Wales. The most obvious of those distinctions is the rate and volume of serious violent crimes— the sort of offenses most likely to result (almost anywhere in the world) in lengthy prison sentences. Allow me to illustrate what I mean.

In 2018, Germany experienced 2,471 homicides (a data point that reflects both murder and manslaughter). Germany's 2018 population was approximately 83.2 million. In the year ending in March 2018, England and Wales experienced 726 homicides and had a population of approximately 59 million. That's 3,197 homicides spread across these countries with a combined population of approximately 142.2 million people.

Now let's compare those numbers with just a handful of American neighborhoods.

In 2018, four contiguous community areas on Chicago's West Side (Austin, East Garfield Park, West Garfield Park, and Humboldt Park) experienced 121 homicides, despite housing just 189,846 people. That same year, Baltimore's Western and Southwestern police districts, with an estimated population of 103,052, experienced 100 homicides. Detroit's 8th and 9th precincts (home to 160,354) had 81 homicides in 2018. Add three St. Louis neighborhoods with a combined population of just 19,352 (the Greater Ville, Wells-Goodfellow, and Baden), and you get 34 additional homicides.[12]

This means that in 2018, just a few slices of just four American cities saw more than 10.5 percent of the homicides seen in the whole of England and Wales and Germany that year, despite housing just 0.33 percent of the combined population of those countries.

This gap in homicide victimization rates goes a long way toward explaining America's comparatively higher incarceration rate, particularly given the fact that many of the countries we are unfavorably compared to respond equally punitively to homicide convicts who constitute a significant slice of our prison population. For example, as recently as 1992, Germany sentenced a slightly higher percentage of those convicted of willful homicide to lengthy prison sentences than did the US, with 14 percent of those convicted in Germany being sentenced to life versus just 9 percent being sentenced to life here.[13] This is a dated statistic, to be sure. But then again, Germany's sentencing practices in response to homicide have remained remarkably stable over time.[14]

For another example of how other countries can be equally or even more punitive in response to certain offenses, consider that in the United Kingdom, "The mandatory minimum sentence for those aged 18 and over [and caught with an illegal firearm] is five years' imprisonment, and three years for those aged 16–17 years,"[15] whereas the median amount of time served by state prisoners primarily in for a weapons offense here in the US is just 15 months.[16] Weapons offenses account for similar percentages of the UK's and US's adult prison populations,[17] but with somewhere in the range of 400 million firearms in the US,[18] compared to just 4 million in the UK,[19] the US simply has a greater number of gun offenders.

Another important disparity between the US and the rest of the world is wealth. More specifically, I'm referring to our outsized ability to spend on our law enforcement apparatuses—policing, prosecution, and incarceration. It stands to reason that the comparably lower imprisonment rate of a country like Brazil (which has a significantly larger violent crime problem than the United States) is more likely due to differences in the resources deployed toward law enforcement than disparities in punitiveness.[20]

Taking account of these important differences is an essential first step for anyone seeking to have a more than superficial understanding of why the United States is an international outlier when it comes to incarceration.

## CAN MASS DECARCERATION BE CONGRUENT WITH PUBLIC SAFETY? NO.

Let's start with prisons.

In assessing the downside risk that a mass decarceration effort would pose, it makes sense to start with an overview of who actually goes to prison in the United States.

Despite all you've probably heard about "draconian" prison sentences being handed down to low-level, nonviolent offenders, the inescapable reality is this: Post-conviction imprisonment is usually a relatively short-term sanction mostly reserved for violent and/or repeat offenders that are highly likely to reoffend once released. And while there is certainly a subset of the prison population whose incarceration does not serve a legitimate penological end, it is a small one. There is simply no way to decarcerate on a "mass" scale without releasing and also refusing to incarcerate scores upon scores upon scores of serious violent offenders who will continue to victimize members of communities that, frankly, already face enough challenges. This is made clear by the data.

The first thing to know here is that post-conviction imprisonments are not the most common outcome of a state felony conviction. Studies done by the US Department of Justice (DOJ) between 2003 and 2009 show that a clear minority (40 percent) of state felony convictions were of defendants subsequently sent to prison as a result.[21] I'm focusing here on state convictions because, per the Bureau of Justice Statistics (BJS), as of 2019— the most recent year for which data were available as of this writing—about 88 percent of prisoners in the US were under state (as opposed to federal) jurisdiction.[22]

The second thing to know is that the 40 percent of state felony convictions that do result in a prison sentence mostly involve relatively young male offenders who have lengthy criminal histories and/or have been convicted of serious violent crimes.

Just under 93 percent of state prisoners are men, and more than half (56.2 percent) of prisoners are under the age of 40. A quarter (24.9 percent) of them are under 30.[23]

The average number of prior arrests for cohorts of state prisoners released in 2005, 2008, and 2012 ranged between 10.6 and 12.1.[24] The median number of prior arrests for those cohorts ranged between 7.8 and 9.0. The average number of prior convictions for those cohorts of released state prisoners ranged between 4.9 and 5.8, while the median ranged between 3.1 and 5.0. In other words, the vast majority of people in prison have received more than one "second chance," which suggests that not only that three-strikes rules are rarely applied, but also, as criminologist John J. Dilulio Jr. famously put it in 1996, "It's the Hard Core Doing Hard Time."[25]

As of December 31, 2018, more than 60 percent of state prisoners (who, again, constitute nearly 9 out of every 10 of those imprisoned in the US) were primarily incarcerated for (that is, their most serious offense was listed as) a violent (55.5 percent) or weapons (4.6 percent) offense.[26] In fact, just four violent offense categories—murder (14.2 percent), rape/sexual assault (13 percent), robbery (12.4 percent), and aggravated/simple assault (10.9 percent)—account for more than half (50.5 percent) of state prisoners. Notwithstanding the widely held belief that incarceration is driven by the drug war, just 14.1 percent of state prisoners were incarcerated primarily for a drug offense, and the vast majority of them were in primarily for trafficking, as opposed to possession—an offense category that constitutes less than 4 percent of the state prison population.

Notice that these statistics refer to the most serious offenses for which these prisoners are incarcerated. By "most serious offense," the Bureau of Justice Statistics is referring to "the offense with the greatest statutory-maximum sentence."[27] This is important to keep in mind when you hear people talking about so-called nonviolent or drug offenders. It's very possible that many of the prisoners captured by this data were convicted of multiple offenses—which means that at least some of those listed by the BJS as "drug offenders" could also have been convicted of, say, a weapons or other violent offense that did not carry as hefty a sentence as the drug offense for which they were convicted. Another thing to keep in mind is that these BJS statistics are based on the offenses for which prisoners were actually convicted, which may not necessarily reflect the conduct they actually engaged in. Somewhere in the range of 95 percent of state criminal cases are resolved via plea bargain.[28] Plea bargains very often involve, among other things, prosecutors dropping or reducing the severity of the charges a particular defendant is facing in exchange for that defendant's guilty plea. This means that the offenses listed in official accounts of the prison population will often understate the conduct engaged in by a given prisoner.

Even though we've established that most state prisoners are young men with lengthy criminal histories who have been convicted of a violent offense, the data on the time prisoners actually serve show that these individuals don't spend much time in penitentiaries before they're released on parole. A BJS report on state prisoners released in 2018 shows that the median amount of time served is about 15 months.[29] For those whose most serious commitment offense was violent, the median amount of time served was less than two and a half years. For drug offenders, the median was just 12 months. In all, 42 percent of state prisoners were released in less than a year; one in five were released less than six months into their sentences.[30] Even 30 percent of convicted murderers and 64 percent of convicted rapists/sexual assailants were out in less than 10 years.[31] Contrary to the widespread belief that we regularly lock offenders away and throw away the key thanks to so-called truth-in-sentencing regimes, the average state prisoner serves just 44 percent of his sentence before he is released.[32]

IN PART BECAUSE MULTIYEAR prison stints are so rare, somewhere in the range of 95 percent of prisoners will eventually be released, with about 80 percent of those releases being onto parole.[33] Unfortunately, however, the vast majority of those released will go on to reoffend.

Consider the longitudinal studies of recidivism among released state prisoners done by the BJS over the last several years. Looking at cohorts of state prisoners released across 24 to 34 (depending on the study) states in 2005, 2008, and 2012, those studies document the tragically high rate of recidivism among state prisoners. Within five years of their initial releases, between 70.8 percent and 77 percent of inmates reoffend—i.e., are rearrested at least once.[34] But, as the studies of the 2005 and 2008 cohorts show, extending the observation period beyond five years captures quite a bit of additional criminal activity. Those studies have observation periods of 9 and 10 years, respectively. Here are a few of the things they tell us.

While the percentage of prisoners rearrested is generally higher for the younger members of the cohorts than it is for the older members, reflecting a broad trend in the criminological literature—looking at the 2008 cohort, it's worth noting that, at year 10, a clear majority (between 56.1 and 89.5 percent) of prisoners in every age group except those 65 or older generated at least one post-release arrest.[35] This is important, because some reformers will speak about older inmates as if their age reduces their risk of reoffending to near zero. This is undermined by the fact that 40 percent of the prisoners who were 65 or older at the time of their release were rearrested at least once.[36]

On the whole, a whopping 81.9 percent[37] of the 2008 cohort and 83.4 percent[38] of the 2005 cohort recidivated during observation periods of 10 and 9 years, respectively. Just under 40 percent of both cohorts were rearrested for crimes of violence.[39] Over the 10-year observation period, the 2008 cohort of approximately 409,300 prisoners generated approximately 2,197,000 arrests—an average of 5.4 arrests per prisoner over the decade.[40] Over a 9-year observation period, the 2005 cohort of 401,288 prisoners generated an estimated 1,994,000 arrests—an average of 5.0 arrests per prisoner.

Since I've focused this chapter on state prisoners, it's worth noting that federal prisoners also reoffend at troublingly high rates. A 2016 US Sentencing Commission study of recidivism among federal prisoners released in 2005 found that half had been rearrested over an 8-year observation period, with rearrest rates increasing with the severity of a given prisoner's criminal history.[41] Because the federal government's jurisdiction over criminal activity is more limited, the risk that federal offenders pose to the public can vary. For example, federal prisoners primarily incarcerated for firearms-related offenses and robbery were most likely to be rearrested post-release.[42] A 2019 Sentencing

Commission study of recidivism among federal firearms offenders found that those prisoners were rearrested for new crimes at a much higher rate (68.1 percent) than non-firearms offenders.[43] Weapons offenses accounted for 18.5 percent of federal prisoners in 2019.[44]

The reason I'm spending so much time documenting the extremely high likelihood that a released American prisoner will reoffend is to make crystal clear what it is those who advocate for mass decarceration and prison abolition are inviting more of.

Troubling as they are, the data on the recidivism and criminal histories of prisoners don't even fully capture the breadth of the problem of pre- and post-release offending. Why? Two reasons: Most crimes aren't even reported to the police, and the vast majority of crimes that are reported go unsolved and therefore unpunished. As such, things are actually far worse than the official recidivism statistics suggest.

According to the BJS's 2020 report on criminal victimizations, only "[a]bout 40% of violent victimizations and 33% of property victimizations were reported to police in 2020."[45] What's more, just 45.5 percent of the four violent index felony offenses tracked by the FBI (murder/non-negligent manslaughter, robbery, rape, and aggravated assault) were cleared by arrest, and just 17.2 percent of four property index felony offenses tracked by the FBI (burglary, larceny theft, motor vehicle theft, and arson) were cleared by arrest.[46]

Many reformers have argued that the steep decline in crime experienced throughout the country since the mid-1990s should have been accompanied by a similarly sharp decline in our incarceration rate. But when you couple the underreporting of crime with low clearance rates, the flaws in this argument become apparent. Among those flaws is the argument's assumption that the mid-twentieth-century ratio of incarceration to crime was ideal. Decarceration advocates understandably focus on the subset of the prison population that *doesn't* belong behind bars, but what they don't grapple with is the larger subset of the general population that *does*.

Rather than coming up with an abstract ideal rate of incarceration based on the crime rate, we should be seeking to simply do a better job of identifying and releasing the unnecessarily incarcerated while apprehending and incarcerating the unjustifiably free. That a higher number of crimes results in incarceration today than did in years past does not constitute evidence of overincarceration today insofar as it leaves open the possibility that we would have been better off incarcerating a greater share of offenders during those earlier years.

In addition to informing what we can expect to result from any successful effort to decarcerate by 40–50 percent (as has been proposed by various reformers,)[47] the recidivism studies also provide us with a useful reminder of a reality often overlooked when it comes to so-called drug and nonviolent offenders, who receive outsized attention in policy debates. That reality is this: Criminals don't really specialize. As the late great James Q. Wilson put it in *Thinking about Crime*, "Today's robber can be tomorrow's burglar and the next day's car thief."[48] The studies of the 2005 and 2008 released prisoner cohorts done by the BJS show that between 75 and 77 percent of those whose most serious commitment offense was drug-related went on to be rearrested for a nondrug crime.[49] As to both cohorts, more than a third of so-called drug offenders and 40 percent of property offenders were rearrested for at least one violent post-release offense.[50]

The application of categorical labels like "nonviolent" or "drug offender" to prisoners based on their most serious commitment offenses elides the substantial diversity of offenses prisoners have committed and will go on to commit over the course of their criminal careers. Another data point illustrative of this reality comes from the city of Baltimore, whose police department released data on 2017 murder suspects, which showed that seven in 10 of them had at least one prior drug offense in their criminal histories.[51]

The nonspecialization of criminals is why Wilson wrote that "the nature of the present offense" is "not a good clue" to the risk an individual offender poses to the community if released.[52] Incarceration, Wilson argued, is a resource that is most rationally used selectively—that is, when longer terms are reserved "primarily" for "those who, when free, commit the most crimes."[53] At the time, the concept of scientific risk assessment was in its early stages of development. But Wilson seemed to have a positive view of the approach, which would weigh factors like age, drug use, criminal history, and employment history to determine whether an individual was a high-rate offender for whom a longer term of incarceration was warranted.[54]

Failure or unwillingness to incapacitate—through the imposition of appropriately lengthy incarceration terms—serious and high-rate offenders is, and has long been, a major driver of America's crime problem. That failure or unwillingness is partly illustrated by the recidivism data, as well as by the lengthy criminal histories of the hundreds of thousands of people being released from prisons every year. But it's also illustrated by the share of serious violent crime committed by repeat offenders—especially those on probation, parole, or pretrial release.

According to a BJS study of violent felons convicted in large urban counties between 1990 and 2002, 37 percent of convicted violent felons "had an active criminal justice status at the time of their offense."[55] In other words, it has historically been the case that nearly 40 percent of violent felons were on probation, parole, or pretrial release when they committed their offense. That figure was eerily similar to what the 2017 homicide data released by the Baltimore Police Department showed: Nearly 36 percent of the 118 homicide suspects identified that year were on parole or probation at the time of the offense.[56]

Chicago provides another illustration of this problem. A January 2017 University of Chicago Crime Lab study of gun violence in the city found that of those arrested for homicides or shootings in Chicago in 2015 and 2016, about "90 percent had at least one prior arrest, approximately 50 percent had a prior arrest for a violent crime specifically, and almost 40 percent had a prior gun arrest."[57] On average, someone arrested for a homicide or shooting had nearly 12 prior arrests. Almost 20 percent of Chicago shooters and killers had more than 20 priors.

Now, it's impossible to eliminate completely the problem of serious crimes being committed by repeat offenders—at least without completely upending the important liberties central to American life. But that doesn't mean we can't do a better job of using incarceration to combat crime. What I hope these data make clear is the necessity for improvement on this front.

THE LOGIC OF INCAPACITATING offenders through imprisonment is highly intuitive. If you incarcerate for a term of five years an offender who would commit an average of 10 serious felonies a year, it's not hard to see how that individual's incarceration spared his community from the effects of 50 serious crimes. This is an idea that even the most conservative assessments of the incarceration buildup's role in the post-1990s crime decline lend support to. See, for example, William Spelman's "The Limited Importance of Prison Expansion," which suggested that incarceration was responsible for about 25 percent of the 1990s crime decline.[58] As criminal justice reform advocate and scholar Patrick Sharkey put it in *Uneasy Peace*, "even the staunchest critics of mass incarceration acknowledge that the expansion of the imprisoned population contributed to the decline in violence." On this point, even he concedes, "there is no longer much debate."[59]

Beyond incapacitation, incarceration can also deter crime—an example of which was illustrated by Eric Helland and Alexander Tabarrok in their 2007 paper assessing the impact of California's three-strikes law. What they found was that the regime "significantly reduces felony arrest rates among the class of criminals with two strikes by 17–20 percent."[60] But this was hardly surprising.

That incarceration can produce clear and obvious benefits through incapacitation and deterrence doesn't end the inquiry, however. Just because an uptick in incarceration produced benefits *before* doesn't necessarily mean those same benefits will attach to an increase in incarceration *today*. With each additional person we incarcerate, we get closer to the point of diminishing returns. Beyond that point, we run the risk of costing ourselves more than we're saving. Some decarceration advocates say we've already reached this point, but that's hardly clear given the high rates of recidivism documented above. Now, it's theoretically possible that some of that recidivism is *caused* by incarceration—that the experience of prison itself makes inmates more likely to reoffend upon release by leading them to either strengthen their ties to the criminal underworld or become more comfortable with a criminal lifestyle—and indeed many advocates said just that. But the certainty with which many make this claim isn't justified by the available evidence, which is far more ambiguous than proponents of this view let on.

Does incarceration cause more post-conviction crime than an alternative response to the same offense? If so, how much more recidivism does that lead to? Is it enough to outweigh the incapacitation benefits enjoyed during the period of incarceration? If so, can we reduce those deleterious effects without incurring the risks associated with mass decarceration? These are all questions that proponents of mass decarceration don't have strong answers to—even the ones who claim otherwise.

In her 2019 book, *Prisoners of Politics*, New York University School of Law professor Rachel Barkow asserted that "policies that satiate punitive desires in the short term sometimes come with longer-term hits to public safety,"[61] and accused decarceration opponents of "not car[ing]" that "long terms of incarceration or collateral consequences of conviction prompt more criminal behavior."[62]

While some studies have found imprisonment to have criminogenic effects—that is, have found that incarceration leads to *more* crime post-release than would be committed if a non-incarceration sanction was handed down instead—others, including those with more reliable designs, have found null or even negative (that is, recidivism-reducing) effects. According to a review of the still-developing literature published in the *Annual Review of Criminology*, "most" of the 13 studies assessing "the experience of postconviction imprisonment" found that it "has little impact on the probability of recidivism."[63] That's not exactly what I would call unambiguously definitive. As my Manhattan Institute colleague Robert VerBruggen recently put it in a piece entitled, "How Much Leniency with Criminals Can We Afford?," the major caveat to these papers—those that find incarceration to have significant criminogenic effects—is that they pertain to marginal offenders whose incarceration came down to random factors. In other words, these studies don't tell us much about the typical prisoner who likely poses different risks than the marginal offender.

What's interesting about that review is that it shows that findings of "recidivism-reducing effects are mostly in settings in which rehabilitative programming is emphasized," whereas the findings of "criminogenic effects are found in settings in which such programming is not emphasized."[64] This is a point of interest because, to the extent incarceration has a criminogenic effect, decarceration isn't the only—or the most obvious—solution to that problem. Rather, it seems we should be exploring ways to *reform* incarceration to make it less likely to exacerbate the criminal propensities of inmates—particularly given the risk that decarceration poses to the public's safety. This is an argument that decarceration advocates who cite the potentially criminogenic effect of incarceration accidentally make themselves. An example can be found in a highly acclaimed essay by Ta-Nehisi Coates in *The Atlantic*, wherein he highlights the downside of incarceration by arguing that "the attitude that helps one survive in prison is almost the opposite of the kind needed to make it outside."[65] To bolster this point, he quotes Craig Haney, who observed:

"A tough veneer that precludes seeking help for personal problems, the generalized mistrust that comes from the fear of exploitation, and a tendency to strike out in response to minimal provocations are highly functional in many prison contexts but problematic virtually everywhere else."[66]

If a tendency toward violence is "highly functional" in prison, it's because violence is the language of the people that inhabit prisons, which highlights the dissonance at play in the minds of those who, on the one hand, can clearly observe this reality yet, on the other, maintain that we can release these very same people.

By pushing back on the idea that we should cut prison rolls by 50–75 percent (which is what it would take for the US to achieve parity with other Western European democracies on incarceration), I am *not* saying that imprisonment can't or shouldn't be improved. To the extent we can reduce recidivism through evidence-based rehabilitation and reentry programs, or by making prisons safer and less crowded, *we should*!

Another thing that these studies don't tell us is whether any deleterious effect of imprisonment can be minimized by extending the length of sentences, given that the propensity to criminally offend declines significantly with age.

It's worth noting that the same review of incarceration's effects on recidivism also looked at studies of *pretrial* incarceration, more of which produced findings of criminogenic effects. This is a finding that is often used to argue in support of broad reductions of pretrial detention that would ultimately include high-risk offenders. But most of these don't assess the impact of detention on particularly high-risk defendants, who may already be highly likely to reoffend.

In the fall of 2021, the *New York Times* provided an example of this caveat being overlooked. The paper's editorial board relied on a single study to claim that by jailing people in New York's Rikers Island jail complex, the city was incurring an "absurd expense," given that "some evidence shows that pretrial detention for even a few days makes someone more likely to commit a crime, not less."[67] What the *Times* left out was that the effects observed in the study they cited was driven by the incarceration of *low-risk* defendants. "For *high-risk* defendants" (emphasis added), according to the study, "there was no relationship between pretrial incarceration and increased crime," which, it went on to suggest, meant "that high-risk defendants can be detained before trial without compromising, and in fact enhancing, public safety and the fair administration of justice."[68]

## CONCLUSION

Like many public policy issues, questions about how best to handle post-conviction incarceration are complex. I believe that the majority of those pushing for reforms are, at least for the most part, trying to address real problems that are worthy of serious consideration and our best efforts. Addressing those problems, however, involves trade-offs and requires a balancing of legitimate concerns about justice with equally legitimate concerns about public safety. Unfortunately, supporters of a more radical approach to reform have constructed a narrative around these legitimate concerns in order to push a misguided mass decarceration program, and that narrative is incongruous with the evidence.

While many Americans have been convinced that the US suffers from a mass incarceration problem that requires a mass decarceration solution, the claim just doesn't hold up to scrutiny. International comparisons fall flat given how much more crime the US sees in a given year. And the data on imprisonment *clearly* show that the sanction is reserved for serious offenders with lengthy criminal histories who are very likely to reoffend when released. Does this mean that there aren't any inefficiencies in the system? Of course not. But those inefficiencies don't justify taking the risks inherent in the sorts of cuts to incarceration that many activists have proposed—risks the crime data make clear will fall disproportionately on the shoulders of Black and brown residents in economically disadvantaged urban enclaves.

Many activists have sought to counter this point by highlighting some studies suggesting that incarceration may, at least as to some offenders, lead to more crime than it prevents. Considering the possibility that incarceration imposes costs that should be weighed against the crime reduction effects enjoyed primarily through the incapacitation and deterrence benefits of incarceration is a more than valid enterprise. But at least as of now, the activists are overstating the evidence on this point.

The push to decarcerate extends beyond prisons and includes plans to reduce the populations of our jails. This has led to a host of other reforms specifically aimed at this population. The more radical arguments in favor of drastically cutting back on pretrial detention often reflect serious analytical errors but nevertheless deserve their own hearing.

# CHAPTER THREE

# AGAINST MASS DECARCERATION,
## PART 2: PRETRIAL DETENTION

While the previous chapter focused on the debate about how to deal with prisoners who've been convicted of the crimes for which they've been incarcerated, there is a parallel debate going on regarding how we should deal with those who have been charged but not yet convicted.

Of the 2 million or so individuals incarcerated in the US on a given day, approximately 631,000 of them are *jail* inmates, and nearly three-quarters of those people are awaiting the disposition of their cases.[1] This is not a small number. As such, many decarceration efforts have been directed at reducing the jail population, as well as the prison population. The most popular (and successful) of those reform efforts are those aimed at reducing or eliminating the use of cash bail.

The need for pretrial detention reforms is real, but reforms must be pursued soberly and with eyes wide open to the risks associated with drastic changes to pretrial release practices.

In the interest of facilitating a more productive bail reform debate, this chapter is going to make three points:

1. Pretrial justice systems that rely heavily on monetary conditions on release—that is, cash bail—can and sometimes do place undue burdens on individual liberty, highlighting the need for reform.

2. Reform in this space should be approached with an eye toward mitigating the risks associated with eroding the incapacitation benefits that can be attributed to pretrial detention (particularly with respect to high-risk, high-rate offenders), which, it seems, can be done best by utilizing and refining algorithmic risk assessment tools.

3. Because much of the concern surrounding the issue of bail reform is rooted in the amount of time presumably innocent defendants stand to spend in pretrial detention (which, in turn, is almost entirely a question of resources), more attention has to be given to the question of how budgetary policy can facilitate the quicker, more efficient processing of criminal cases at the state and local level— particularly through the hiring of more judges, prosecutors, and public defenders.

Typically, when an individual is arrested and charged with a crime, they are brought before a judge who will decide whether and under what conditions they will be released while their case runs its course. In jurisdictions that allow for the imposition of cash bail, the judge can, at least in some cases, require the defendant to post "a security such as cash or a bond . . . required by a court for the release of a prisoner who must appear in court at a future time."[2] Depending on the jurisdiction, that requirement can be based on the judge's assessment of the risk that the defendant will fail to appear for his next court date, or that they will reoffend during the pretrial period.

When a judge imposes bail, the defendant can either pay the court in cash—which is then held in escrow and returned upon the defendant's return to court—or secure a bail bond by paying a bondsman a percentage of the bail amount.[3] Basic economics teaches us that raising the price of anything will, at least in theory, price some people out of the particular market in question. Bail is no different. As such, in jurisdictions in which judges can impose financial conditions on a given defendant's release, there will inevitably be cases in which some defendants will be financially unable to post bail or secure a bail bond. Unless the bail amount is lowered to the point of affordability, or unless someone else fronts the money, defendants who are financially unable to satisfy monetary conditions on their release will remain in pretrial detention. This is where the concerns animating so many proponents of bail reform begin to arise.

One of the most persuasive arguments against pretrial justice systems that rely heavily on cash bail is that such systems would allow for a dangerous but well-off defendant to secure their release, while a poor but harmless defendant would remain in pretrial detention for an extended period of time. In other words, the problem with relying heavily on cash bail is that it makes the question of pretrial release one of means rather than one of risk.[4] Such outcomes are unjust, and avoiding them is a proper aim of a bail reform effort.

Such outcomes are more prevalent in some jurisdictions than others. In New York City—where I've resided most of my life— prolonged pretrial detentions have not been typical for some time.

In 2018 (before the state enacted a sweeping bail reform measure that took effect on January 1, 2020), less than 14 percent of the more than 250,000 individuals arrested by New York City police had bail set in their cases. Approximately 10 percent entered a city jail due to a failure to make bail after their initial court appearance. Of that 10 percent almost half made bail within two days, 70 percent did so within a week, and another 17 percent did so within a month. A 2019 analysis of pretrial detention done by the Mayor's Office of Criminal Justice found that of the more than 257,865 individuals whose arrests were captured by that report, 43 percent (110,915) of defendants were released on their own recognizance at their initial hearing, and 1.8 percent (4,720) were released under supervision. Another 42.7 percent (110,110) of the total had their cases resolved (either through dismissal or a plea) soon after their arrests (prior to the opportunity to have bail set), and 1.5 percent (3,940) of defendants made bail at their initial appearance. Of the remaining 11 percent (28,180)—representing defendants who entered jail—0.7 percent (1,830) were ordered held without bail, and 10.3 percent (26,350) entered jail as a result of not making bail at their initial court appearance.[5]

The thing to keep in mind about New York, which makes it unique, is that judges are prohibited from considering the danger a given defendant poses to the community at every stage and in every aspect of pretrial release decisions.[6] This is important because not every defendant detained pretrial on account of his inability to make bail should or would have been released if New York judges were allowed to consider public safety when making release decisions.

However, as with almost any public policy decision, bail reform involves trade-offs. On one side of the scale, you have the defendant's liberty. On the other, you have the public's safety. Expanding pretrial release for its own sake inherently raises the risks to the public's safety, just as restricting pretrial release for its own sake raises the risks to the liberty of criminal defendants. Because so much concern and attention have been directed toward mitigating the latter risk, I'd like to focus a bit on the former.

One thing the research on bail reform seems to show pretty convincingly is that an increase in the percentage of pretrial defendants released pending trial will translate to more crimes committed by that population. One study by researchers at Princeton, Harvard, and Stanford Universities found that pretrial release increased the likelihood of rearrest prior to case disposition by more than 37 percent.[7] It also increased the likelihood of a defendant failing to appear in court by 124 percent, which adds to the burden of police officers tasked with returning absconders to court. Two other studies analyzing the recent bail reform effort in Chicago also found increases in the number of crimes committed by pretrial defendants in that jurisdiction.

The first study, by University of Utah professors Paul Cassell and Richard Fowles, found this: "Properly measured and estimated, after more generous release procedures were put in place, the number of released defendants charged with committing new crimes increased by 45%. And, more concerning, the number of pretrial releasees charged with committing new violent crimes increased by an estimated 33%."[8] The second study, by Loyola University professors Don Stemen and David Olson, found that pretrial releasees reoffended at the same rate prior to and after the bail reform went into effect, and that during the study period, approximately 500 additional pretrial defendants were released pursuant to the reform effort.[9] As my Manhattan Institute colleague Charles Fain Lehman pointed out in his coverage of the latter study, "[T]he 9,200 individuals released following reform committed roughly 1,573 crimes and 294 violent crimes. If only 8,700 offenders had been released, they'd have committed 1,488 new crimes and 278 violent crimes. In other words, the release of just 500 people led to roughly 85 additional crimes, including 16 additional violent crimes."[10]

It's also worth noting that in a study cited in the previous chapter of violent felons convicted in large urban counties, the Bureau of Justice Statistics found that 12 percent of felons over the 12-year study period were out on pretrial release at the time of their arrests.[11]

To put a finer point on the public safety stakes of this debate, consider the story of 16-year-old Kahlik Grier, who was shot and killed in January 2021 in the Bronx while in the stairwell of his own apartment building.[12] One of the people charged with his murder was a 19-year-old suspect named Desire Louree, who, according to news reports, had been released from jail after making bail a month prior to the shooting. At the time of Grier's death, reports stated that Louree had open cases for gun possession and attempted murder—the former from 2019, and the latter stemming from a 2020 shooting in Brooklyn.[13] Consider also the case of Arjun Tyler, another New York City defendant who allegedly attempted to rape a woman in Brooklyn not long after being released from pretrial detention pursuant to New York's relatively recent bail reform.[14]

Their alleged victims also have liberty interests that should be given due consideration in debates about bail reform. Minimizing the risks faced by those with the highest likelihood of being victimized by pretrial defendants who reoffend is as worthy a cause as protecting the liberty interests of the accused.

How to balance those interests is not an easy question.

Maintaining cash bail would minimize some of the risks associated with expansions of pretrial release because some subset of those detained as a result of their inability to pay would have reoffended. But this is both an inefficient and unjust way to approach mitigating the risks associated with expansions of pretrial release.

In my estimation, a better approach is to structure reforms in such a way that empowers judges to remand dangerous or high-risk offenders to pretrial detention, irrespective of the charges they face. Many presume that the offenses with which a defendant is charged in the instant case are a reliable indicator of the risk that they pose to the public during the pretrial period. They're not. According to a study by the New York City Criminal Justice Agency, "the likelihood of (a failure to appear) and/or re-arrest for a violent offense was lower among defendants initially arrested for felony-level violent and property offenses" than it was "among defendants initially arrested for all types of misdemeanor or lesser offenses."[15] While this may seem counterintuitive to some, many high-risk offenders often engage in a broad range of misconduct. So it's not only possible, but likely, for a high-risk offender to be arrested for what would generally be regarded as a low-level offense.

This was a point highlighted by my late colleague George L. Kelling, who noted the following in an article about community policing:

Responding to the subway disorder [in the 1990s] had early and unexpected benefits. Transit police found that one out of every seven fare-evaders was wanted on a warrant, while one out of 21 was carrying a weapon. Cops called it the "Cracker Jack box" effect. Kids would buy a box of the caramel-covered popcorn snack for the toy inside as much as for the popcorn itself; when it came to enforcing laws against fare evasion, the "toy"—the thing that made the effort even more worthwhile, for both the cops and the public—was the weapon or wanted criminal taken off the street.[16]

A fairer and more accurate way for judges to assess a given defendant's risk is through a validated algorithmic risk assessment tool (RAT), which calculates risk based on attaching weights to a variety of factors like criminal history and age. A recent study by the Center for Court Innovation illustrated the predictive accuracy of such a tool—even across racial groups, which is a crucial criterion, given the opposition of some reformers who claim that racial bias is built into the algorithms.[17] It's worth noting, however, that in New York City, courts have been using an algorithmic RAT to assess flight risk for years—a practice that was left undisturbed by the 2020 bail reform and its 2021 amendment. Also, in jurisdictions that recently enacted bail reforms (such as New Jersey), the use of RATs hasn't materially changed the racial composition of the jail population.

To be clear, it is possible because of how heavily many RATs weigh criminal history that an assessment of "erroneous"[18] classifications would reveal that when Black defendants (who tend to have more extensive criminal histories compared with white defendants)[19] are misclassified, they are more likely to be misclassified as high-risk than defendants of other races. Nevertheless, implementing an algorithmic RAT to inform judicial assessments of the dangers that defendants pose to their communities will provide judges with a more objective framework to aid them in their pretrial release decisions—one that is far preferable to having them set bail with the hope that dangerous defendants can't come up with the money.

That said, RATs do not have to be the be-all, end-all of the pretrial release decision. Judges should maintain the discretion to consider case-specific evidence that both the prosecution and the defense bring to light, particularly if that evidence can contextualize the risk assessment before them. For example, consider this hypothetical: A defendant who, due to his age and criminal history, scored quite high on an algorithmic RAT was recently paralyzed in a car accident. Judges should probably not be constrained to remand pursuant to the RAT, given the defendant's incapacitating injury. In other words, RATs should be considered highly probative pieces of a bigger body of evidence that ought to be considered in its totality.

Some critics, not unreasonably, highlight the tension between the presumption of innocence and the pretrial detention of a defendant who has not yet been convicted. That tension is very real. However, I would be remiss not to note that the Constitution does not require forbidding the latter to serve the former—something the Supreme Court has held on multiple occasions.[20] Minimizing that tension between safety concerns and the presumption of innocence is a public policy problem that, unlike most policy issues, is almost purely a matter of resource allocation.

Simply put, a better-funded criminal justice system that can afford more prosecutors, public defenders, investigators, and judges is the most direct route to shortening pretrial detention periods, as well as ensuring that the Constitution's guarantee of a speedy trial is fulfilled in all cases. Notably, the state of New Jersey's bail reform capped the pretrial detention period at 180 days and set aside funding for 20 new superior court judgeships to help move cases along.[21] A real effort to assess how much capacity needs to be added to speed up the resolution of cases is the first step toward a long-term solution to many of the issues surrounding criminal prosecutions. Here is where the federal government may be able to play the role of facilitator by directing funds to states and localities whose criminal justice systems are most severely underfunded so that defendants in those jurisdictions will spend as little time in pretrial detention as possible.

## CONCLUSION

There are plenty of good reasons to be concerned by the unfortunate reality that some people get stuck behind bars for months at a time without having been duly convicted of the crimes they've been charged with. But those concerns have to be weighed against society's legitimate interest in maintaining and promoting public safety. This chapter argues that a better balance can be achieved by reorienting the pretrial release inquiry around an objective assessment of risk instead of a defendant's ability to come up with some amount of money set according to a schedule that doesn't take into consideration any of the relevant factors unique to the defendant before the judge in question.

Unfortunately, many jurisdictions have taken a different route, simply choosing to implement sweeping reforms aimed at reducing the jail population for its own sake. Mounting evidence suggests that these efforts have done real harm to the public's safety—a point that activists have sought to counter by overstating evidence of collateral consequences and other harms associated with incarceration.

One of the other costs of incarceration often highlighted by reform advocates is the deleterious impact that it can have on the children of those incarcerated. But as you'll see in chapter 4, this too is far from clear.

# CHAPTER FOUR

# THE MORE COMPLICATED STORY OF INCARCERATION AND THE FAMILY

Back in 1983, on the PBS show *Firing Line*, Thomas Sowell said the following to the show's original host, William F. Buckley, during a discussion about his brilliant book *The Economics and Politics of Race: An International Perspective*:[1] "If you are born into . . . a family, where there are certain values—and particularly if they are families that really insist upon those values, where it's not a matter of doing your own thing—then you will grow up with those values; and you will have whatever the benefits that happen to come along with those values."

My reading of the available evidence (some of which has been quite effectively presented by Sowell himself) led me to conclude some years ago that he was exactly right. In that *Firing Line* segment, Sowell was talking specifically about the values, attitudes, and behaviors associated with economic and social advancement. But what if his argument also holds true as to values, attitudes, and behaviors associated with all manner of observable phenomena, including economic and social decline?

In other words, if the prosocial behaviors typically engaged in by the family someone is born into will almost certainly be engaged in by that person, it stands to reason that a family in which antisocial behaviors are engaged in at high rates will be more likely to fail to properly socialize the children within it, increasing the likelihood that those children will become antisocial adults.

A viral incident from the summer of 2019 brought Sowell's comments to mind. The incident offers a disturbing glimpse into what children see and hear—and what they might go on to learn and mimic. Imagine for a moment that you're scrolling through your favorite social media app (as I was that summer), and you come across a widely shared video of one family's trip to Mickey's Toontown, inside California's Disneyland. You click on it with the expectation of seeing a touching interaction between some young lad and his favorite character. Instead, it begins with a man in a red shirt arguing with and cursing at a woman standing next to another man while holding on to a stroller into which two small children are strapped. Things boil over. The woman spits at the man in the red shirt, who then repeatedly hits her in the face before setting his sights on her male companion. The two men square up and briefly trade blows, each taking at least one break to strike each other's female companions.

Awful, right? Well, it's not over yet. The female companion of the red-shirted man begins fighting with the woman who spat on him. Their children can be seen and heard crying in the background. At one point in the nearly four-minute ordeal, an older woman struggles out of her electric wheelchair, trying to get between the two younger women. She gets knocked to the ground and needs to be helped up.

The older woman, it turns out, is the mother of the man in the red shirt. Upon learning that his female companion had (albeit inadvertently) knocked his mother to the ground, the red-shirted man, who had seemed to be calming down, now assaults his own female companion—but not before repeatedly striking the woman with whom he was originally arguing, who is apparently his own sister. Only then did other patrons at last intervene, putting an end to the violent episode.

So where am I going with this?

One of the most rhetorically potent arguments in favor of drastically cutting incarceration is that incarceration deprives families—particularly children—of the economic and emotional support of the parent(s) or sibling(s) removed from their homes or everyday lives.

In the title of a 2015 lecture on "the ripple effects of mass incarceration," criminal justice reform advocate Jeremy Travis asked, "What about the children?"[2] The importance of this question for Travis was, in part, a function of the reality that talking about "the children" is, as he put it, a "well-known tactic for building broad political coalitions." Other advocates saw the same potential.

In a compendium of essays on mass incarceration published by the Brennan Center for Justice at New York University, Black Lives Matter co-founder Alicia Garza wrote, "More than 2.3 million people are incarcerated in the United States . . . That's 2.3 million families that have been torn apart."[3] In that same compendium, Van Jones, cofounder of the #cut50 initiative to reduce the incarcerated population by half, made similar claims. In addition to "perpetuating the ugly legacy of racism," argued Jones, imprisonment is "tearing families apart."[4]

"Tearing families apart" is a common refrain invoked often by reform advocates in support of decarceration efforts.[5]

In the lead up to the 2020 presidential election, many of the Democratic Party candidates echoed those arguments. In her criminal justice reform plan, Senator Elizabeth Warren lamented that "one in ten Black children has an incarcerated parent."[6] Then candidate Joe Biden suggested allowing "nonviolent offenders who are primary care providers for their children to serve their sentences through in-home monitoring"[7]—a proposal clearly intended to address the problem that "children with incarcerated parents tend to do worse in school, experience anxiety and depression, and develop behavioral issues," as Bernie Sanders put it when he was still vying to be the nation's chief executive.[8]

Understandably, arguments about the potential effects of parental incarceration on children have resonated with some Republicans and conservative-leaning thinkers too. In a 2015 speech delivered at the Heritage Foundation, Senator Mike Lee, a Republican from Utah, observed that "a majority of prisoners are also parents—most of whom lived with their minor children before they were arrested or incarcerated."[9] He found fault with a "penitentiary approach to punishment" that "severs the offenders' ties to their family."[10] Writing in a *National Affairs* piece titled "The Conservative Case for Jail Reform," Arthur Rizer (then the R Street Institute's director of criminal justice) noted that "Incarceration separates offenders from their families, which increases rates of homelessness and single parenthood.

"Approximately 17 million children are currently being raised without a father, a growing social problem that only perpetuates cycles of violence and crime," Rizer wrote.[11]

These ideas are also subscribed to by some who operate much closer to America's criminal justice system than pundits and federal lawmakers[12]—indeed, by many working at the very center of the system. Brooklyn district attorney and self-styled "progressive prosecutor" Eric Gonzalez assured Brooklynites in a document laying out his office's Justice 2020 initiative that his approach would reflect his belief that incarceration has "had the effect of destabilizing families."[13]

Even some judges seem to have bought in to this as well. On October 4, 2019, NYPD officers responded to an alert from the city's ShotSpotter system, which reports shootings directly to police. Officers alleged they arrived at the shooting scene in time to observe 32-year-old Shakeil Chandler kicking a .357 Magnum revolver under a car. They arrested him for illegal weapons possession. Like so many of those charged with serious violent offenses, Chandler was no stranger to the criminal justice system. According to the *New York Post*, he was a reputed member of the Crips and had served nearly a decade in prison for a manslaughter conviction stemming from a 2006 shooting in Queens before getting paroled in 2014.[14] Though aware of Chandler's history, Bronx criminal court judge Jeanine Johnson released him without bail, citing a recommendation by the New York City Criminal Justice Agency and noting that he had "full custody of his child."[15]

When I read the news story about Chandler's arrest, I remembered asking myself how on earth a reputed gang member with such a violent criminal history even wound up with full custody of a child. But more to the point of this chapter, I also wondered whether it had ever occurred to this judge that she might be doing Chandler's child a disservice by not locking Chandler up.

THE SMALL HANDFUL OF guys I grew up with who ended up doing time all had one thing in common: Their biological dads weren't around. They weren't all absent because of prison. In most of their cases, the paternal absence owed to other things. Nevertheless, the fact that their dads weren't around would seem to lend support to the theory that child-parent separation due to incarceration exacerbates the risks of those children falling into lives of crime.

Generally speaking, there is no question that two parents are better than one, and it seems pretty clear that fathers play an important role—as role models, authority figures, and so forth—in the development of their children. Nor does it strain credulity to accept that seeing a parent or sibling hauled off to jail in handcuffs can be incredibly traumatic for any child. Those of us engaged in the public debate about how our society ought to respond to crime should certainly keep this in mind, which means recognizing that the children affected by the incarceration of their parents or siblings deserve our compassion.

But true compassion cannot be understood as requiring us to allow policy decisions to be driven by broad generalizations or the emotions certain unfortunate realities evoke. Hard as it may be for some to read, the idea that criminal justice policy should by default aim to keep criminal offenders involved in the everyday lives of their families rests on a yet unproven assumption: that the sort of people who tend to find themselves behind bars by and large are (or can be) good parents—that is, reliable sources of economic and emotional support whose presence in a child's life produces benefits that outweigh the costs of that parent's absence.

The evidentiary basis for this assumption is shaky. In fact, considerable evidence suggests that the struggles of children whose parents get incarcerated—whether in school or in other areas of their lives—have less to do with their parents being incarcerated than with the underlying behavioral patterns that led to the incarceration. If that's true, then decarceration motivated by concerns about parental separation might turn out to be a move with serious unintended consequences that actually end up hurting the very children reformers say they're trying to help.

Think of it this way: Being raised by both Philip and Vivian Banks—the model parents played by James Avery and Janet Hubert (and later Daphne Maxwell Reid) on the 1990s sitcom *The Fresh Prince of Bel-Air*—would be clearly ideal for most kids. Falling far short of that ideal would be a virtual certainty if you replaced Philip Banks with, say, Tony Soprano—the ruthless, narcissistic gangster at the center of HBO's hit series *The Sopranos*. This chapter is concerned primarily with the question of whether those who argue society should adopt a presumption in favor of allowing criminal parents (including those who rank below New Jersey mafia bosses in the hierarchy of the criminal underworld) to remain in their homes for the sake of their children (rather than be incarcerated) are right. In other words, are the reform advocates quoted above correct to assume that, on net, the presence of even a criminal parent is beneficial enough for their children that the presumption of judges and prosecutors ought to be *against* that parent's incarceration?

Whether a parent's presence in a child's life is beneficial seems heavily dependent on whether that parent engages in high levels of antisocial behavior—behaviors generally reflecting, among other things, a failure to conform to social norms, deceitfulness, impulsivity, reckless disregard for others, high levels of irritability and aggressiveness, and remorselessness in the wake of misbehavior. The literature on the intergenerational transmission of antisocial behavior suggests that the presence of parents who engage in such behavior may be even worse for a child than the absence of a pro-social parent. "Fathers' antisocial behaviors predicted growth in children's externalizing and internalizing behavior problems, with links stronger among resident-father families," according to a study published in the *Journal of Abnormal Child Psychology*.[16] These results, the study's authors warned, "suggest caution in policies and programs which seek to universally increase marriage or father involvement without attention to fathers' behaviors."[17]

That finding squares with earlier work led by Sara Jaffee, a professor of psychology at the University of Pennsylvania and lead author of a paper published in the journal *Child Development*, which found that the "quality of a father's involvement matters more than his mere presence," and that children who live with fathers who "engage in very high levels of antisocial behavior" will go on to behave "significantly worse" than "their peers whose fathers also engage in high levels of antisocial behavior but do not reside with their children."[18] Jaffee and her coauthors added that the "advantages of growing up in a two-parent family may be negated when one or both parents are characterized by a history of antisocial behavior."[19]

This makes perfect sense and probably strikes most people who take a few moments to think about it as intuitively obvious. Intuitive as it may be once you've heard it explained, the logical appeal of this idea escapes many.

Exposure to highly antisocial parents—perhaps the sort who don't think twice about throwing haymakers at

Disneyland—increases the likelihood that a child will develop serious conduct problems, which, according to Jaffee and her coauthors, "are the strongest predictor of a range of adverse outcomes in adolescence and adulthood . . . including school dropout, teen childbearing, crime, and unemployment."[20] As researchers Zachary Torry and Stephen Billick put it in a research paper published in *Psychiatric Quarterly*, antisocial parents can damage "a child's emotional, cognitive, and social development" and leave them "traumatized, empty, and incapable of forming meaningful personal relationships."[21] Such exposure seems to also be criminogenic for children—that is, it increases the likelihood that they'll later engage in criminal behavior, feeding an all-too-visible cycle of crime and violence plaguing so many of the country's most vulnerable neighborhoods.

Consider a 2018 study published in the *Journal of the American Academy of Child and Adolescent Psychiatry*, which looked at 227 sets of identical twins and found that "the twin who received harsher parenting had higher aggression and more [callous-unemotional (CU)] traits," and that "the twin receiving warmer parenting evidenced lower CU traits."[22] This is important insofar as it responds to the argument that such behavioral disorders in children are driven mostly by genetics. While genes obviously play a role (as they do in so many aspects of life), the evidence seems to overwhelmingly support the conclusion that the environment can both mitigate and exacerbate the risks posed by children predisposed toward aggression. A paper published in the *Journal of Clinical Child Psychology* in 2000 strongly linked physically aggressive parenting with childhood aggression.[23] The paper went on to suggest that parenting practices were predictive of "oppositional and aggressive behavior problems."[24] And the predictiveness of parenting practices, according to the study, "were fairly consistent across ethnic groups and sex."[25]

The next question, then, is whether there's significant overlap between the kinds of men who engage in high levels of antisocial behavior and those who often find themselves behind bars. The answer appears to be a resounding yes. As Jaffee and her coauthors, observe, "high-antisocial fathers were significantly more likely to meet" the criterion for a clinical diagnosis of antisocial personality disorder (ASPD). And ASPD, it turns out, has long been common among prison inmates. It's also worth pointing out that the red-shirted man at Disneyland is alleged to have a "multistate criminal history," according to news sources citing the judge who allegedly denied the red-shirted man's request for a lower bail shortly after the viral incident.[26]

According to a 2002 article in *The Lancet*, nearly half of just under 19,000 male prisoners surveyed across 12 countries had ASPD.[27] That survey found that prisoners were "about ten times more likely to have antisocial personality disorder than the general population"[28]—an estimate that might *understate* the prevalence. A 2016 article in *Translational Psychiatry* noted that while only between 1 and 3 percent of the general public have ASPD, the disorder has a prevalence of "40–70 percent in prison populations."[29]

An interesting thread in the research on ASPD among prisoners is the prevalence of comorbidity with—that is, the simultaneous presence of—substance use disorders (SUDs). A study published in the *Annals of Clinical Psychiatry* found that "offenders with ASPD are much more likely to have other types of mental illness," including high rates of substance use.[30] Moreover, offenders with ASPD and comorbid SUDs seem to have worse outcomes than offenders with only ASPD. A Spanish study suggests that inmates with both ASPD and a SUD exhibit a "tendency to carry out more aggressive crimes."[31] A 2008 study of patients making threats against others found that the "highest risks [for subsequent violence] were in substance misusers."[32] Another notes that psychiatric patients with "various personality disorders and comorbid substance abuse . . . represent a high risk group for violence within forensic psychiatric facilities, and repetitive violent behavior in the community."[33]

What makes these findings so important is that drug offenders (especially users) have been such a keen focus of anti-incarceration reformers, who argue that responding to addiction and its outgrowths through the criminal justice system is wrong. A 2016 report titled "The Human Toll of Criminalizing Drug Use in the United States" by Human Rights Watch "recount[ed] how harmful the long-term consequences of incarceration and a criminal record that follow a conviction for drug possession can be."[34] First among the harms listed was "separating parents from young children."[35] What the paper doesn't seem to consider is the possibility that separating young children from at least some drug offenders can help children more than it hurts them.

SO FAR, I'VE HIGHLIGHTED evidence that exposure to highly antisocial fathers is extremely detrimental for children and associated with a host of negative life outcomes, from the development of behavioral disorders and other psychological problems to poor educational outcomes and criminality in later life. I've highlighted studies showing that ASPD is *very* common in carceral settings and that when ASPD is accompanied by a substance use disorder, the mix can be especially dangerous. All of this makes for a pretty good reason to be suspicious of the claim that incarceration should be universally assumed to be detrimental (compared to a noncarceral sanction) for the children of those placed in the state's custody. What makes that suspicion even stronger, however, is a developing body of research testing this very question.

"Contrary to conventional wisdom," according to a 2021 paper published in the *American Economic Review*, "parental incarceration has beneficial effects on children, reducing their likelihood of incarceration by 4.9 percentage points and improving their adult socioeconomic status." The authors also found that "Sibling incarceration leads to similar reductions in criminal activity." The paper, "The Effects of Parental and Sibling Incarceration: Evidence from Ohio," was coauthored by researchers at the University of Chicago, UC Berkeley, and the University of Southern California. They studied a sample of children with parents on the margins of incarceration—that is, whether they were incarcerated depended heavily on the leniency or severity of the judges handling their cases. They measured not only the life-outcome differences between the children with incarcerated parents or siblings and those without, but also the portion of those differences attributable to the incarcerations.

The authors highlight several potential explanations for why children might benefit from a family member's incarceration, which differed depending on whether the incarcerated family member was a parent or a sibling. The study found that the benefits of parental incarceration for children owed less to the parent's removal than to the deterrent effect on the child of witnessing the levying of criminal sanctions firsthand. That finding could, however, reflect that the parents in the sample were mostly facing lower-level drug and property offenses; the removal effect—that is, the impact attributable to the parent's absence—in cases involving more serious criminal conduct could be more pronounced. Contrasted with the effects of parental incarceration, the positive effects of a sibling's incarceration were "concentrated almost exclusively in the short term"—that is, "while the sibling is still incarcerated." This, the authors noted, "reflects that the removal of a criminogenic influence—as opposed to deterrence—is the more important mechanism [in cases of sibling incarceration], potentially because siblings can strongly influence one another towards or away from criminal activity."

These findings resemble those from other studies done in the United States and elsewhere. In a study of incarcerated parents in North Carolina, University of Colorado professor Stephen Billings found that "removing negative potential role models through incarceration benefits children"—particularly in terms of their performance and behavior at school.[36] A paper looking at data out of Norway estimated "a 32 percentage point reduction over a four year period in the probability a younger brother will be charged with a crime if his older brother is incarcerated."[37] In a 2018 study of incarceration in Colombia, economist Carolina Arteaga found that "conditional on conviction, parental incarceration increases years of education by 0.8 years for children whose parents are on the margin of incarceration."[38]

AND WHILE THE APPARENT *psychological* effects of antisocial and criminal parents on children's life outcomes are compelling, we should remember that sometimes the system's failure to separate a criminal parent from their child(ren) can lead to *physical* harm due to both abuse and neglect. I came across a particularly disturbing example of the former while watching bodycam footage of police shootings for a piece I was working on a couple of years ago.

The video—which depicted the 2019 fatal police shooting of a woman in Henderson, Nevada—began with the audio recording of a bloodcurdling 911 call placed by the woman who was eventually killed.[39] A child could be heard crying in the background as his mother gave the dispatcher their address in a chillingly calm tone. The boy interjected within seconds, "My mom is trying to kill me!" The mother confirmed, "They're making us do it." Clearly, it seemed to me as I listened, this woman was either in a state of psychosis or on a bad trip. "911 help me!" the child screamed again in the background. He could be heard frantically begging, "Don't hurt me, please! Don't hurt me! . . . Please! You help me! . . . Mommy don't!" Then the line went dead.

Two officers arrived at the address given and knocked on the door of an apartment. Out walked a little boy, just six years old, completely silent, shirtless, and bloodied with apparent stab wounds. "Hello—Whoa! Whoa, whoa, oh shit. Get medical," said the officer at the door to his partner waiting at the bottom of the stairway leading to the ground level. Not far behind the boy was his naked mother, later identified as Claudia Rodriguez-Mendez, who promptly initiated a struggle with the officer at the door. They fell to the ground, at which point she was able to take control of his sidearm and squeeze off a round as the two struggled over the gun, prompting his partner to run in and fatally shoot Rodriguez-Mendez.

The Clark County district attorney issued a report detailing the evidence and concluding that the shooting was justified.[40] It included photos of the apartment, which was covered in the boy's blood. After the shooting, the officers begin tending to the boy, who repeatedly told officers that he was going to die and that his mom tried to kill him, pausing at one point to vomit. Thankfully, the boy survived. However, it's clear that this was not the first time Rodriguez-Mendez had put her unfitness for parenthood on display. Local news reports noted that she had been arrested at least four times in the four years prior to the almost deadly attack on her young son, all for domestic violence.[41] She was convicted in one of those cases and had another pending at the time of the shooting. So, you might be wondering, why on earth was she at home with that boy? The answer, it seems, can probably be found in the same argument that has been driving the dual pursuits of mass decarceration and depolicing as public policy goods unto themselves.

## CONCLUSION

At the very least, the research outlined in this chapter undermines the assumptions of those who oppose parental incarceration, insisting that it causes harm to the children of criminal parents. Yet mass decarceration advocates seem as resolute as ever. Indeed, when the study of parental incarceration in Ohio was published in the *American Economic Review* in the spring of 2021, it caused what Bloomberg opinion writer Noah Smith described as "a torrent of negative reactions" from academics and the broader Twitterverse. According to some of them, ethical considerations should outweigh whatever benefits might attend the publication of findings that undermine the push for decarceration. But this is the sort of disposition at the root of much of the criminal injustices American cities have seen more and more of in the last few years—that is, at the root of the countless examples of innocents paying for the second, third, and fifteenth chances of offenders with their lives. Unless they are stood up to, a more moderate approach will be hard to implement—which could very well mean, perhaps ironically, that more children will suffer more than they otherwise would have.

# CHAPTER FIVE

# USE OF FORCE AND THE PRACTICAL LIMITS OF POPULAR POLICE REFORMS

Policing has spent quite a bit of time front and center in contemporary debates about criminal justice, perhaps even more so than incarceration. Police reform has always been a heavy, complex, and politically fraught topic. But after the murder of George Floyd by Minneapolis police officer Derek Chauvin, our national conversation about policing and race reached something of a fever pitch—one that brought to mind both past and recent uprisings in the wake of viral police uses of force. While rare, national turmoil in the wake of a viral police use of force incident is not unheard of. Examples throughout the country's history include the infamous Watts riots outside Los Angeles in 1965, the 1992 riots that followed the acquittal of the police officers indicted for beating Rodney King in Los Angeles, as well as the more recent protests and riots that followed the deaths of Michael Brown in Ferguson, Missouri; Eric Garner in Staten Island, New York; Freddie Gray in Baltimore; and Laquan McDonald in Chicago.

What makes the post-Floyd period different than previous public outcries about police use of force is that politicians across the country began a mad dash to their respective legislative chambers in order to make increasingly sweeping policy changes ranging from reasonable to radical. The race down Reform Road was not visibly stymied by the fact that the nation saw its largest ever single-year homicide spike in 2020.

In April 2021, the *New York Times* reported that since the death of George Floyd, "Over 30 states have passed more than 140 new police oversight and reform laws," citing the paper's own analysis of data provided by the National Conference of State Legislatures.[1] Lest you think all the action was at the state level, city councils and local politicians were also doing their part to reform policing and criminal justice practices. Just weeks after Floyd's murder, the Minneapolis city council, for example, voted unanimously to dismantle the city's police department,[2] and New York's city council enacted a package of reforms in March 2021 that included, among other things, provisions aimed at increasing the likelihood of police officers being held personally liable when sued for actions taken in the field, prohibiting cops from living outside the city limits (despite an ongoing recruitment and retention crisis), and turning officer discipline over to a civilian complaint review board.[3] This was in addition to the council's criminalization of officers applying pressure to the backs, necks, or diaphragms of suspects while making arrests in 2020—a law that was later struck down as unconstitutionally vague.[4]

The tone of our police reform debate is as toxic as I've ever heard it, and that toxicity is more likely to cloud our collective judgement than it is to illuminate a more sensible approach. In this chapter I attempt to clarify some of the key terms of this debate.

Before I do so, however, let me acknowledge that "police reform" is a somewhat amorphous term that can refer to a large number of policy changes. I couldn't possibly cover them all in a single chapter. Generally, I use the term as a reference to rules and regulations aimed at constraining police power and/or restricting various types of police activity—all with the overarching goal of reducing police uses of force. Rather than try to cover everything that might fall under that definition, this chapter will examine five broad proposals that have received a lot of attention in our ongoing national debate, highlighting the practical limits of these proposals.

In referring to a particular proposal's limits, I'm referring to my assessment of a given proposal's ability to, if enacted, significantly reduce police uses of force and do so without significantly harming the public's safety. There are two reasons I'm focusing on these two particular implications of the proposals this chapter will cover: First, police uses of force constitute the main reason police reform has dominated public policy conversations since May 2020. So it's only right that we evaluate the potential for a given reform to make force less common. Second, one of the biggest risks of tinkering with policing and criminal justice policies is that of serious crime going up, and the social costs of additional crime are not trivial. In other words, as we consider the proposals evaluated in this chapter, we should do so with the understanding that a measure that will succeed at reducing police uses of force should nevertheless be rejected if the same proposal will likely create more harm than it abates through its impact on crime.

The five broad proposals this chapter will consider are defunding the police, demilitarizing the police, abolishing qualified immunity, recommitting to de-escalation training, and diverting certain calls for service away from police to mental health responders.

Each of these proposals, as I see it, suffers from at least one of two practical limits on its ability to significantly (and safely) reduce police uses of force—particularly deadly force. The first of these limits lies in the data on police use of force, which, in their proper context, illustrate just how rarely police actually use physical force—meaning that there is much less room for improvement than one might guess after consuming the mainstream media narrative about policing in America. The second of these practical limits lies in what the relevant literature has to say about these proposals.

Before digging into the actual proposals, however, it's necessary to say a few more words about the first of the two practical limits outlined above.

## THE DATA IN CONTEXT

Between 2015 and 2020, police in the US shot and killed an average of 993 people a year.[5] That police kill almost 1,000 people a year is a statistic many understandably find jarring, but context is important. Viewing the number of fatal police shootings in its proper context undercuts the claim—which is central to the case for the reforms discussed later on—that America has a police violence problem.

This is not to say that police never use excessive force. Nor is it to assert that there isn't any room for improvements in police training and tactics that might, at least at the margins, reduce use of force incidents. But to the extent the prevalence of unjustifiable police violence is overstated, so too will be the potential impact of any policy levers pulled to address that problem. This matters, because the advisability of a given policy proposal depends in part on how much will change (and in what direction) should the policy be adopted.

Again, there is no question that every year there are many documented instances of excessive police force that are individually problematic. However, to establish that the institution of policing has a violence problem, one must be able to demonstrate that such individual incidents are actually representative of a larger pattern. The data on police shootings and other uses of force simply don't support that conclusion.

Let's take a look at some pre-pandemic numbers. According to the *Washington Post*'s database of fatal police shootings, there were 990 such shootings in 2018.[6] It's worth noting that approximately 93 percent of those shootings involved armed suspects, according to the database, which includes just 58 shootings of unarmed suspects and 11 shootings of suspects whom the *Post* could not verify as being either armed or unarmed. Of course, fatal police shootings are only a subset of total police shootings, which includes incidents in which suspects survive their wounds, as well incidents in which suspects are shot at but not hit. In order to get a more complete picture of how many times police purposefully discharged their firearms in 2018, I analyzed a Vice News dataset of police shootings by officers working in the nation's 50 largest local police agencies over a six-year period for a law review article I published in 2020.[7] The analysis found a total of 3,936 shootings, 1,284 (or 32.6 percent) of which were fatal. Based on that breakdown, let's assume for argument's sake that the 990 fatal shootings documented by the *Washington Post* in 2018 constitute 32.6 percent of total firearms discharges by police that year. That would mean that police in 2018 purposefully discharged their firearms 3,037 times—more than eight shootings a day, which is probably an overestimation. That sounds like far too many at first glance, but the initial shock should fade once you contextualize that number in light of the overall volume of police activity that year.

Per the Uniform Crime Reporting Program of the Federal Bureau of Investigation (FBI), there were an estimated 686,665 full-time police officers working in the United States in 2018.[8] That year, American cops made 10,310,960 arrests,[9] which constitute only a fraction of the total number of contacts police have with the public, such as traffic and pedestrian stops. The Bureau of Justice Statistics (BJS) reported that in 2018, police had contact with 61.5 million individuals over the age of 16.[10] And it stands to reason that some will have had multiple contacts with police.

These data must be incorporated into any honest analysis of police uses of force. Even if we were to attribute each of the 3,037 estimated police shootings in 2018 to a unique officer, we would only be able to say that, at most, just 0.44 percent of police officers purposefully discharged their firearms that year, and if we were to assume that every one of those 3,037 estimated shootings happened within the course of a separate arrest, we would only be able to say that, at most, just 0.03 percent of arrests resulted in a police shooting. These numbers simply don't match the rhetoric that has long animated the police reform movement. An example of this was provided by NBA superstar LeBron James, who told reporters in 2020 that Black people in the United States feel like police are "hunting us."[11] For another example, consider the American Civil Liberties Union's use of the word "epidemic" to describe police shootings in the US.[12]

The case for a national police violence problem doesn't get much stronger when we move on from deadly force to the data on nondeadly force. The BJS report on police contacts with the public in 2018 shows that just 2.8 percent of the 31.1 million people with whom the police initiated contact were subjected to the use or threat of force.[13] Just 0.3 percent of those individuals reported having a gun pointed or fired at them.[14] Another BJS study covering the 10-year period between 2002 and 2011 found that just 0.8 percent of people who had contact with police reported actually being subjected to (as opposed to just threatened with) physical force.[15]

In 2018, a research team of doctors and a criminologist published a study of police uses of force in the *Journal of Trauma and Acute Care Surgery* titled "Injuries Associated with Police Use-of-Force."[16] The study analyzed more than 1 million calls for service, which resulted in more than 114,000 criminal arrests effected by officers in three midsized police departments—one in North Carolina, one in Arizona, and one in Louisiana. The findings are instructive. Police officers used physical force in just 1 in every 128 of those arrests, meaning that more than 99 percent of those arrests were completed without the use of any force whatsoever. Moreover, based on expert medical examinations of the medical records of arrestees, the study went on to find that 98 percent of the suspects subjected to physical force "sustained no or mild injury." Only 1.8 percent of suspects sustained moderate or severe injuries, and only one fatal police shooting was captured by the analysis.

What the data outlined above show is that although there are a lot of use-of-force incidents, viewing those incidents in their proper context reveals that use of physical force is nevertheless an extremely unlikely outcome of a given interaction with the police. Another important piece of context is that many, if not most, police uses of force are justified. Incidents of excessive force are a small subset of the whole. It's admittedly difficult to accurately disaggregate justifiable from unjustifiable uses of force in the publicly available data, but there are some instructive scholarly estimates that have been published over the years.

A BJS study of 2002 data on citizen complaints filed against American police officers in departments with at least 100 full-time sworn personnel found that just 8 percent of the force complaints for which there was a final disposition were sustained. Police critics might be dismissive of this number, viewing it as merely an illustration of the unwillingness of police administrators to hold their officers accountable. Fair enough. But I would note that the same study shows an even smaller percentage (just 6 percent) of complaints being substantiated in jurisdictions that task a civilian complaint review board (CCRB) with such dispositions. The BJS study arrived at an estimated rate of excessive force of just one incident per 200 full-time sworn officers.[17] This is in line with data out of my home city of New York. In 2018, New York City's CCRB received a total of 4,475 complaints, just 226 (5 percent) of which were substantiated against 326 (of the department's approximately 36,000) officers. Just under 3,000 (2,919) of the complaints contained allegations of excessive physical force; and just 73 (2.5 percent) of those allegations were substantiated.[18] Keep in mind that in 2018, the NYPD made

245,392 arrests,[19] to say nothing of the other enforcement-related encounters such as pedestrian and traffic stops.

Here's the thing: Cops are human. As such, even the most competent and well-intentioned of officers will fall short of perfection—a standard to which no human being can be fairly held. Even the most expensive, highly precise Swiss timepieces are expected to lose or gain a few seconds per day.[20] Yet some of the harshest police critics seem to be guilty of blurring the line between imperfection and deficiency. The question isn't whether cops will make mistakes. Of course they will. Beyond mistakes, some uses of force will inevitably reflect wanton recklessness and even criminal malevolence.

The question I want you to ask yourself is this: In the context of almost 700,000 officers making more than 10 million arrests and conducting tens of millions of traffic and pedestrian stops every year, can you honestly say that the data on uses of force establish an institutional police violence problem? I don't see how one can answer that question in the affirmative. If I'm right, then as things already stand, there isn't a whole lot of room for a massive reduction in police violence. I don't say this to argue that reform is not worth pursuing; rather, I make this point to encourage you, the reader, to be sober and realistic about just how much we can expect to reduce an already exceedingly rare occurrence.

Now on to those proposals . . .

## DON'T DEFUND THE POLICE!

There is one reform proposal—which has received a lot of attention since 2020—that has the potential to put a large dent in police use of force numbers: defunding the police. The problem is, though, that the empirical literature on the effect of police on crime makes overwhelmingly clear that pulling this particular policy lever will result in the deaths of a hell of a lot more people than police kill.

If I had to summarize one of the most consistent and robust findings in the criminological literature in a single sentence, it would go something like this: More policing means less crime. A reasonable inference to draw from that finding is that significantly depolicing will mean more crime. Of course, it's a bit more complicated than that, but the main idea remains the same. Consider some examples.

In 2005, economists Jonathan Klick and Alexander Tabarrok found a strong causal connection between police presence and crime, showing that the latter declined when the former was boosted.[21] They looked at how police presence along the National Mall in Washington, DC, changed as a result of changes in the terror threat alert level, and assessed how those changes affected crime in and around the National Mall. What they found was that "an increase in police presence of about 50 percent leads to a statistically and economically significant decrease in crime on the order of 16 percent."

In another study, Klick, along with criminologist John MacDonald and law professor Ben Grunwald, found that an increase in private police patrols around the University of Pennsylvania "decreased crime in adjacent city blocks by 43%–73%."[22] In yet another analysis, University of Pennsylvania criminologist Aaron Chalfin, along with law professor Justin McCrary, found "reduced victim costs of $1.63 for each additional dollar spent on police in 2010, implying that U.S. cities are under-policed."[23]

That incredibly impressive rate of return was driven largely by the effect policing has on murder—a crime with incredibly high social costs.

Chalfin, in a paper coauthored with other economists who study crime, found not just that "Each additional police officer abates approximately 0.1 homicides," but also that "In per capita terms, effects are twice as large for Black versus white victims."[24] This, as this book's final chapter will explore, is an empirical reality that is in tension with the idea that depolicing will somehow advance the interests of Black Americans who, I would remind you, are many times—ten times, in the case of Black men—more likely than their white counterparts to be homicide victims.

These are just but a few of many empirical analyses showing how more (and more proactive) policing can reduce crime. But it's also worth noting that there are also analyses which suggest that less policing can lead to more crime. A good example is a 2020 paper coauthored by Harvard economists Tanaya Devi and Roland Fryer that assessed the impact of federal "pattern and practice" investigations—investigations into whether police departments were engaging in unconstitutional discrimination—on crime.[25] Devi and Fryer found that the investigations launched in the wake of viral police use of force incidents "led to a large and statistically significant increase in homicides and total crime." How much of an increase? In five cities, "these investigations caused almost 900 excess homicides and almost 34,000 excess felonies," during the two-year study period. You may be wondering how a federal investigation causes that kind of crime spike. Well, according to Devi and Fryer, the most viable explanation "is an abrupt change in the quantity of policing activity." In other words, sharp declines in police–citizen interactions—which ranged in magnitude from

46 percent to 90 percent—are the most likely drivers of hundreds upon hundreds of lives lost and tens of thousands of additional victimizations of all stripes.

Having said all that, let me once again acknowledge that cops are fallible. Some are downright evil. Only the truly naïve would refuse to acknowledge that some cops have gotten (and will get) drunk on the power that comes with a government-issued badge and gun. But you can find evil lurking in every corner of the earth—in every profession, in every institution. Nevertheless, police have extraordinary powers that set them apart from others. As such, it's only fair they be held to standards that reflect this reality, and it's absolutely essential that when police fall short of those standards, they are held accountable. The question is how we achieve that without tipping the scales away from justice— that is, without leaving our society vulnerable to the evil that police are meant to protect us from. Defunding them clearly isn't the answer. So let's look at a few other proposals.

## "MILITARIZATION" ISN'T DRIVING USE OF FORCE

Unfortunately, George Floyd was not the only person to become a household name in the spring of 2020. During a warrant service operation gone wrong, police in Louisville, Kentucky, shot and killed Breonna Taylor, who quickly became one of the central characters in the media and political narratives built around the deaths of other Black Americans at the hands of police. Taylor was shot after her boyfriend, Kenneth Walker, opened fire on police, wounding one of the officers serving the search warrant. Walker apparently believed that the police were intruders when he opened fire, but that prompted police to shoot back, hitting and killing Taylor, who was apparently standing beside Walker.

The initial news coverage quickly focused on the fact that police were granted what's called a no-knock warrant, which allows those serving it to forcefully enter the dwelling in question without knocking and announcing themselves. The city of Louisville subsequently banned no-knock warrants in legislation named for Taylor.[26]

In theory and in practice, no-knock warrants can give police a tactical advantage when confronting dangerous suspects and can also minimize the risk of evidence destruction. That, however, doesn't mean they aren't over- or misused. More on that later.

In addition to calls to defund the police, Breonna Taylor's tragic death also resparked calls to demilitarize the police. Efforts to establish a police militarization problem are often based on an alleged overreliance on no-knock warrants and an overuse of heavily armed special weapons and tactics (SWAT) teams. Critics charge that both of these phenomena contribute to the police violence problem. Here again, however, the available evidence is at odds with the claim underlying the reform proposals related to militarization, which include curtailing the use of SWAT teams, cutting off the supply to local police departments of surplus military equipment from the federal government, and banning no-knock warrants.

Let's start with SWAT teams. In a 2008 study prepared for the US Department of Justice's National Institute of Justice, criminologists David A. Klinger and Jeff Rojek "estimated that across the *hundreds of team years* for which [there was] data that SWAT officers took suspects under fire in just 342 of the tens of thousands of operations they undertook"[27] (emphasis added).

The NYPD's Emergency Service Unit (ESU—our SWAT team equivalent) officers recorded just three on-duty shootings during the four-year period of 2017–2020.[28] In Chicago, SWAT teams filed just 26 (approximately 0.003 percent) of the department's 10,068 Tactical Response Reports—which the department requires officers to file whenever they're involved in reportable uses of force, which range from takedowns and strikes to the discharges of Tasers and firearms—filed in 2017 and 2018.[29] During that two-year period, Chicago SWAT officers were involved in just four (4.5 percent) of the department's 88 reported discharges.[30] Even the ACLU, in a 2014 study on police militarization, reported that only five of the 818 SWAT raids evaluated resulted in a fatal police shooting.[31]

There is no denying that SWAT teams have indeed become more prevalent and more commonly used across American police departments over the last several decades. But the numbers mentioned above seem to suggest that they account for an infinitesimal share of serious police uses of force. This is an important point because critics like *Washington Post* columnist Radley Balko often cite the rise of SWAT teams (along with the escalation of the War on Drugs) in the late 1960s and early 1970s as the drivers of police "militarization," which has been suggested as one of the causes of our alleged police violence problem.[32]

In addition to the fact that SWAT teams don't seem to be responsible for much of the force police actually use, there is another data point that seems incongruous with the claim that the militarization of policing since the 1970s has contributed to the overuse of force by cops: the drastic decline in police uses of force since the 1970s. Take, for example, the trend of officer-involved shootings within the NYPD. In 1971, NYPD officers shot and injured 221 people; in 1972, that number was 145.[33] In 1990, the number had gone down to 72, and in 2019, NYPD officers shot and injured just 13 suspects.[34] Let's take a look at Chicago, where police shot and wounded 523 civilians between 1974 and 1978—about 100 people a year.[35] Fast-forward to 2019, and you get a total of 34 firearm discharges.[36] In 2019, LAPD officers recorded 26 officer-involved shootings, which was down from 115 in 1990[37]—a period in which, we're told, departments across the country became increasingly militarized.

Just as SWAT teams don't seem to play all that large of a role in use of force incidents, there doesn't seem to be much to the claim that by outfitting local cops with surplus military equipment—rifles, body armor, armored personnel carriers, and so forth—the federal government has created a network of violent Frankensteins.

For years, the US Department of Defense has administered what has come to be known as the 1033 program, through which tribal, state, and local law enforcement agencies can obtain surplus military equipment. That program, however, garnered quite a bit of negative attention after the very public display of military style equipment by heavily armed police forces during the riots in Ferguson, Missouri, that followed the fatal shooting of Michael Brown. That display was quickly followed by calls to do away with the program, prompting President Barack Obama to order a review of the program's scope.[38]

The intense public debate about the wisdom of providing police with equipment some felt had no place outside of a war zone also prompted researchers to scrutinize the program for any connection between its administration and police uses of force. Those analyses, by and large, do not support the placement of limits on the ability of police to acquire and use military surplus equipment as a mechanism through which to meaningfully reduce use of force incidents.

Many critics of the program often rely heavily on a 2017 study of the program's effects which did find "a positive and statistically significant relationship between 1033 transfers and fatalities from officer-involved shootings."[39] But that analysis, which its authors acknowledged was "relatively preliminary," is based on county-level data in just four states (Connecticut, Maine, Nevada, and New Hampshire). What's more, this finding is contradicted by three subsequent empirical assessments of the 1033 program. One—a working paper—was undertaken by Olugbenga Ajilore, a senior economist at the far-left Center for American Progress, who found "little evidence of a causal link between general military surplus equipment and documented use-of-force incidents."[40]

Another assessment of the program by researchers at the University of Tennessee used a much larger sample of police agencies than the 2017 study mentioned above and failed to find any effect on police shootings. It did find that certain 1033 acquisitions actually "reduced citizen complaints," as well as "assaults on and deaths of police officers."[41]

A third study—which was published in the same issue of the same journal as the one just mentioned—concluded that 1033 transfers had "no effect on the number of offenders killed" by police.[42] The analysis went on to find that the 1033 program proved to have a cost-effective deterrent effect on crime that was achieved primarily through the mechanism of deterrence. According to the study's authors, "two highly visible tools, gears and vehicles, have strong and sizeable effects on all the types of crime," which, they explained, "is consistent with earlier studies . . . which explore how police wearing military-style uniforms influences citizens' perception of the police's authority and legitimacy, and reinforces the notion that a main causal channel could be based on perceptual deterrence."

In short, it does not seem to be the case that police violence can be significantly reduced by limiting the use of SWAT teams or the access officers have to certain types of equipment. In fact, pulling those particular policy levers may actually make both police and suspects marginally less safe. That doesn't mean every reform proposed by those concerned about police militarization should be rejected. No-knock warrants are a good example, despite the fact that they rarely result in death.

In mid-2020 Vox's Dara Lind reported that police conduct somewhere in the range of 20,000 no-knock raids per year.[43] Police militarization critic Radley Balko of the *Washington Post* estimated on NPR in June 2020 that approximately 40 people are killed annually during such raids.[44] It is plausible that these types of unannounced dynamic entry operations might increase the chances of someone inside the dwelling being raided mistakenly believing that his or her home was being broken into. And, in a country whose citizens retain (and regularly exercise) the right to keep and bear arms for self-defense (more than 40 percent of Americans have reported either owning or living with someone who owns a firearm),[45] such a mistake can prove deadly for those on both sides of the door. One can also imagine instances in which the element of surprise might maximize officer safety. Therefore, an outright ban on no-knock raids is probably a step too far. A better approach might be for departments to condition no-knock warrant requests on the detailed written approval of an executive officer tasked with evaluating (preferably on the basis of actual intelligence) the tactical necessity of an unannounced entry.

The point about actual intelligence is key because a failure on the part of police departments to do their homework can lead to tragedy. Consider a raid undertaken by SWAT officers in Wisconsin who threw a flashbang grenade into the bedroom of Alecia and Bounkham Phonesavanh.[46] The flashbang landed in the playpen of the couple's 18-month-old baby, who suffered a collapsed lung and severe burns, requiring the baby to be kept in a medically induced coma for more than a month. The target of the warrant was not even home at the time police made their entry. Police should have surveilled the residence not only to confirm the presence of their target in the home but also to get an idea of where in the house he might be. Had they done that, they could have avoided changing an innocent child's life forever.

So, even assuming that there are levers we should pull in response to the alleged militarization of police forces over the last 50 years, it doesn't seem to be the case that the two most popular proposals (limiting SWAT deployments and cutting off the supply of military grade equipment) would have much of an effect on police uses of force. And while I support modest limits on the practice of unannounced dynamic entries into homes by police, I don't think such a reform would have an impact beyond the margins—which, by the way is perfectly fine, and should not be taken as a reason to refrain from pursuing any reform. A small move in the right direction is still better than nothing. My point here and throughout the rest of this chapter is that we have to be realistic and honest about the likely effects of a given proposal.

## QUALIFIED IMMUNITY ISN'T THE SHIELD SOME SAY IT IS

While I'm sure they'd rather have not gone through their ordeal at all, Alecia and Bounkham Phonesavanh and their child were at least compensated when they settled their legal claims against the police for $3.6 million. Some police critics would have you believe that this family got lucky, because the lawsuit wasn't blocked by qualified immunity—a once obscure (but now much discussed) legal doctrine (an affirmative defense, actually) that protects state actors (not just cops) from being sued in their personal capacities for violating federal constitutional or statutory rights that were not yet established at the time those actors engaged in the conduct in question. One way to think about it is as a protection for government agents against ex post facto liability—a notice requirement, if you will. It's also worth making clear that the defense applies only in cases filed pursuant to section 1983 of title 42 of the US Code, which creates a right of action for those whose federal civil rights established either by the Constitution (say, under the Fourth Amendment) or by the laws of the United States were violated.

Basically, when qualified immunity is asserted, the court will ask whether the officers violated a right that was "clearly established" (usually by a prior case covering a sufficiently similar situation) at the time. If the right being asserted wasn't yet clearly established, then the suit is not allowed to proceed against the individual officers being sued even if the asserted right was violated.

On its face, this rule seems to make sense. After all, it hardly seems fair to bankrupt an officer for conduct—probably undertaken in the heat of the moment and with little time for analysis—that they had no reason to know would constitute a civil rights violation. But there are plenty of examples of courts shielding officers from suits based on clear misconduct on qualified immunity grounds by relying on minor factual distinctions to set the case in question apart from controlling precedents. This gives critics of qualified immunity a legitimate beef, but they've gotten way too far ahead of themselves. Qualified immunity abolitionists argue that these examples reflect a pattern of judicial deference that, in turn, contributes to the internalization of a sense of immunity on the part of police, who then go on to misbehave in ways that they wouldn't if they had more financial skin in the game. However, as you'll see in these next few paragraphs, whatever the demerits of qualified immunity are as a legal question, the role the doctrine plays in both modern police litigation and officer behavior is drastically overstated, raising a real question about just how much use of force trends would change if the doctrine was abolished tomorrow. I suspect the answer is probably not much at all.

Calls to abolish qualified immunity actually garnered significant legislative support in the wake of the deaths of George Floyd and Breonna Taylor, the latter of whom was invoked by Massachusetts congresswoman (and defund supporter[47]) Ayanna Pressley when she introduced legislation to abolish the legal defense. A recent Pew Research poll found significant public support for the idea.[48] And in addition to federal legislative proposals like Pressley's, the state of Colorado passed legislation providing litigants with a way to end-run the defense in that state.[49] New Mexico quickly followed suit,[50] as did New York City, which is no small thing, given that the NYPD is the country's single largest police department by a significant margin.[51]

In addition to being named in proposed federal legislation, Breonna Taylor's case was cited by many commentators in the context of explicit and implicit criticisms of qualified immunity (if not outright calls to abolish the doctrine). In the *New York Times*, Taylor's family attorneys were quoted as saying that getting justice would require them "to overcome an obstacle known as 'qualified immunity.'"[52] The *Washington Post*'s Radley Balko noted in an article on Taylor's death that he had "never come across anyone who has ever won a lawsuit against police officers solely for violating" the knock and announce rule.[53] Throwing cold water on those predictions, the city of Louisville went on to settle Taylor's family's wrongful death suit for $12 million.[54]

In addition to Taylor's name, George Floyd's name was also invoked repeatedly in public calls to abolish qualified immunity—something one might now look askance at given that his family received a $27 million settlement from the city of Minneapolis without having to take the case to trial or overcome as assertion of qualified immunity.[55] Examples of such invocations include a federal proposal that would have abolished qualified immunity called the George Floyd Justice in Policing Act[56] and a strongly worded editorial in the *New York Times* series on George Floyd and America titled "End the Court Doctrine That Enables Police Brutality."[57] The *Times* wasn't just wrong to imply that Floyd's family would have a hard time in court; it was wrong to suggest that qualified immunity is actually driving police behavior. Why? Because the evidence simply doesn't support that claim.

The reality is that seven- or eight-figure payouts to those who've been on the enforcement end of viral use of force incidents are not an exception to a general rule of no compensation; they're essentially the norm. Rodney King received $3.8 million after he was beaten by police during his 1991 arrest in LA. Laquan McDonald's family received a $5 million settlement after his murder by a Chicago police officer in 2016. Stephon Clark's estate received a $2.4 million settlement after he was killed by police in Sacramento in 2018. Kalief Browder's family received $3.3 million after Browder killed himself—a suicide they alleged stemmed from his experiences in New York's Rikers Island jail complex. Tamir Rice's family was paid $6 million. Philando Castile's family got a $3 million settlement. Freddie Gray's family was given $6.4 million. Eric Garner's family settled his case for $5.9 million. And despite multiple investigations concluding that Michael Brown's 2014 shooting in Ferguson, Missouri, was legally justified, his family was given a $1.5 million settlement.[58]

Even when you get beyond the big-name cases, plaintiffs are often (very often) successful in lawsuits alleging police misconduct. The Legal Aid Society maintains a database of lawsuits (2,387 of them) filed against the NYPD between January 2015 and June 2018.[59] Filtering those cases by disposition produces just 74 (3 percent) cases resolved in favor of the police defendants.[60] More than 830 (35 percent) of the cases were settled. The top 10 cases ranked by settlement amount resulted in more than $41.7 million paid out to plaintiffs. These numbers do not seem to indicate that, at least in New York, qualified immunity functions as an effective shield for cops. But perhaps you're not yet convinced.

Consider also an empirical assessment of qualified immunity published in a 2017 issue of the *Yale Law Journal* by UCLA law professor (and noted qualified immunity abolitionist) Joanna C. Schwartz.[61] Her study makes a case against the maintenance of the defense by illustrating that it "rarely serve[s] its intended role as a shield from discovery and trial." Schwartz analyzed more than 1,100 cases filed against state and local law enforcement defendants under section 1983 of title 42 of the US Code. Qualified immunity was a possible defense in 979 (82.8 percent) of those cases, but it was successful (that is, it served as the basis for a partial or whole grant of dismissal or summary judgement) in just 38 cases—3.9 percent of the total. Doesn't sound like much of a shield, does it?

You might be wondering, *Isn't it possible that some substantial number of cases simply don't get filed because lawyers know they'll get tossed?* The answer is yes. It is possible, but there's virtually no evidence of this being the case. Let's go back to Schwartz, who in 2020 published another study in the *Northwestern University Law Review* examining this very question.[62] Schwartz surveyed 94 of the attorneys involved in the cases examined for her 2017 study and conducted in-depth interviews with 35 of them. The findings were, to use her word, "equivocal." The study's ultimate conclusion was this: "Attorneys do not reliably decline cases vulnerable to attack or dismissal on qualified immunity grounds."

So the available evidence suggests that only a small slice of cases are disposed of (or avoided) on qualified immunity grounds, which, to put it lightly, undermines the claim—which, by the way, is at the heart of the movement to abolish qualified immunity for police—that officers see the defense as such a broad shield that it's availability in court enables violent behavior they wouldn't otherwise engage in. That in and of itself is reason to view proposals to limit qualified immunity as severely limited in their capacity to affect police behavior on the ground.

But wait—there's more. It turns out that the defense of qualified immunity isn't even the main source of financial protection for officers. That award goes to something called indemnification—a legal term that essentially means someone else is picking up the tab. In this case, that someone is the taxpayer.

The vast majority of American police officers work in jurisdictions that, pursuant to either collective bargaining agreements or statute, indemnify them against financial liability for damages awarded as a result of actions undertaken within the scope of their employment. In other words, even when officers are successfully sued for money damages, a preexisting agreement usually (indeed, virtually always) requires the municipality or state in question to pay the plaintiff(s) on the officers' behalf, as yet another study from Schwartz shows.[63] Gathering data from 81 large, medium, and small departments around the country, Schwartz's study found that 99.98 percent (virtually every penny) of the dollars paid to plaintiffs were paid by the governments that employed the officers. This is an important point, because at the root of many (though not all) calls to abolish qualified immunity is the belief that the financial protection it offers informs how police behave—a supposition that is completely incongruent with the reality of indemnification, which the abolition of qualified immunity wouldn't change.

All that said, here too there's room for modest reform, even if it won't make a huge difference. As I said at the top of this section, the qualified immunity inquiry has two prongs: Has a right been violated? Was that right clearly established—that is, were the defendants on notice of the right's existence?

A court might answer the first of these questions in the affirmative but still grant immunity by answering the second question in the negative. While this means that the particular plaintiff in that case won't be compensated, the finding as to the first question will establish the right for future cases, such that officers accused of sufficiently similar conduct will no longer be able to succeed in an immunity defense. If courts took this approach, the scope of unestablished rights would shrink relatively rapidly, and we'd run into fewer and fewer instances of plaintiffs being denied compensation despite their rights having been violated. This is exactly what the Supreme Court deemed the "proper sequence" in a 2001 case called *Saucier v. Katz*.[64] Unfortunately, however, the Supreme Court reversed itself eight years later in a case called *Pearson, et al. v. Callahan*,[65] which gave judges the discretion to dispose of cases solely based on whether the right asserted was clearly established by a sufficiently similar prior case—in other words, by skipping the first of the two questions highlighted in the paragraph above. Predictably, lower courts have repeatedly sidestepped the first of those questions ever since. This exacerbates the problem of multiple defendants—sometimes over a period of years—benefiting repeatedly from the resulting underdevelopment of the case law—that is, from the constant sidestepping of the question of whether a right was violated at all.

Rather than doing away with qualified immunity entirely—given that there will be cases in which officers will truly not have been adequately notified about the legal infirmity of their conduct—I've long felt that Congress should consider legislatively reestablishing the rule of *Saucier*. At the very least, this would promote the development of important areas of the law, while also more rapidly shrinking the scope of unestablished rights over time.

## MENTAL HEALTH CALLS AND DE-ESCALATION

If you've ever spent time in a big city like New York or San Francisco, chances are you've witnessed people in the grips of a serious mental illness. Often, those illnesses are exacerbated by drug use. Sometimes, individuals in crisis can become a danger to themselves and those around them. As such, it's not uncommon for police to get calls about men and women in a state of psychosis, who, for one reason or another, have given those in their vicinity reason to fear for their safety or the safety of the individual in crisis. These calls can pose some of the most significant challenges to responding officers, and those difficulties can sometimes lead to police ultimately having to use force to bring the subject under control or repel an attack.

Uses of force involving individuals in the throes of a mental health crisis have informed increasingly loud calls for jurisdictions to both reroute more mental health–related calls away from police to trained mental health professionals and invest more in de-escalation training for officers. There is some support for both ideas in the available literature, but it's not particularly strong. That is, while there is some upside, these proposals don't seem to provide great answers to serious questions about both feasibility and impact. This leads me to believe not only that police will have to continue to respond to mental health calls in high numbers, but also that a rededication to de-escalation training probably won't have more than a marginal effect on serious uses of force. Again, this doesn't mean we shouldn't pull these levers at all. We just shouldn't hold these ideas up as panaceas for what is an incredibly complicated and largely misunderstood issue.

In a strong report published in mid-2021, my Manhattan Institute colleague Charles Fain Lehman reviewed some of the evidence regarding efforts to deploy civilian crisis intervention teams to calls for service involving individuals who seemed to be in crisis.[66] His report concluded that although proposals to remove police from the mental health response game were unsupported by the available evidence, "complementary tools can help relieve stress on overtaxed and understaffed police forces." Among those tools is a popular, oft-cited, and promising effort launched in Eugene, Oregon, called CAHOOTS—an acronym that stands for Crisis Assistance Helping Out on the Streets. While effective, CAHOOTS is also a case study in the limits of programs loosely (and inaccurately) referred to as "alternatives" to policing. As Lehman noted in his report, "CAHOOTS responders are highly specialized. In 2019, they covered just 17% of Eugene 911 calls, with 75% of those calls being a welfare check, providing transportation to someone (usually homeless or in need), or assisting the police already on the beat. Even in those relatively limited circumstances, CAHOOTS responders still called for backup in roughly one in every 67 calls for service in 2019."

It is hard to see that model scaling up to cover two or three times as many 911 calls. Doing so would involve not only dramatically increasing CAHOOTS's $2.1 million budget, but also identifying a large population of trained crisis intervention professionals—and, most significantly, asking those professionals to handle situations that grow increasingly riskier as their responsibilities expand beyond simple welfare checks. In other words, though they doubtless provide a useful service now, groups like CAHOOTS are not a model for how to *replace* the police. As a *complement* to policing, however, it would seem a useful model for other cities to adopt.

There's another wrinkle to consider here: Whether a 911 call can be accurately categorized as one that can be safely diverted away from police to civilian mental health responders is often unclear based on either what's typically communicated to 911 operators or police dispatchers. One study of such calls for service in Philadelphia recently found "that some medical or public health activity initially masquerades as crime or other policing work and some events eventually determined to be police/crime activity can initially appear to be public health related."[67] The study went on to note that "About 20% of activity in this area does not appear predictable from the initial call type as handled by police dispatch."

Before moving on, I want to go back to the point about scale. This is important, because when you consider the sheer volume of mental health-related calls received by police—often in the late-night or early-morning hours, and sometimes on weekends— it becomes clear that the capacity to shift the responsibility of responding to these calls away from police completely simply doesn't exist. In New York City alone, 911 operators field nearly 180,000 calls annually involving emotionally disturbed persons (EDPs, as they're often referred to).[68] That's just one American city. Combine that statistical reality with the fact that in 2017 the US Department of Health and Human Services projected that by 2025, the country would face significant shortages of mental health professionals[69] (clinical psychiatrists, school psychologists, counselors, therapists, social workers, and so forth), and you see just what I mean. There just isn't a pool of qualified people willing to work all hours of the day to respond to volatile situations, many of which will end up requiring the use of force by police anyway. So like it or not, this is a job police are going to continue to do, which provides a good segue into a quick look at what the research says about de-escalation training for cops.

According to a comprehensive field guide outlining best practices for law enforcement published by the US Department of Justice, "Research has identified five attributes common to the clinical literature of de-escalation: communication, self-regulation, assessment, actions, and maintaining safety."[70] The guide—published in 2019—defines these attributes as follows:

1. *Communication* encompasses specific verbal and nonverbal strategies to begin an effective dialogue with an individual and earn that individual's trust and cooperation.

2. *Self-regulation* reflects skills and techniques used by individual service providers to manage their emotional or behavioral responses to an individual encounter. This includes techniques that they can use to provide the subject time and space to cool down.

3. *Assessment* is the task of collecting as much data about the person and situation as possible to make informed decisions about subsequent actions, including understanding when using force becomes imperative.

4. *Actions* refer to the behaviors and activities a service provider can engage in to reduce the likelihood and severity of use of force.

5. *Maintaining safety* describes the paramount need of service providers to ensure their own welfare and public safety. Specific actions can reduce the likelihood that they will be injured if the person becomes violent or coercive methods of control are required.[71]

The guide certainly seems to favor de-escalation training for police officers, but it also acknowledges that "to date, there is still limited empirical literature examining the effects of de-escalation in law enforcement beyond [crisis intervention team training]."[72] That properly identified paucity of research should elicit some skepticism of those who claim that de-escalation techniques can easily and effectively be identified, taught, learned, internalized, and deployed by police in the field with the effect of sharply reducing uses of force.

There is, however, a good bit of work that's been done to assess the effectiveness of de-escalation and crisis intervention training in healthcare settings, which is where comprehensive de-escalation strategies that many hoped could be implemented in law enforcement settings were first developed.[73] That body of work is not particularly encouraging for those holding out hope that a meaningful reduction in police uses of force can be achieved through more significant investments in de-escalation training. Consider this conclusion of a 2015 systematic review of the literature published in the *British Journal of Psychiatry*, which offers little cause for optimism: "It is assumed that [de-escalation] training may improve staff's ability to de-escalate violent and aggressive behaviour. There is currently limited evidence to suggest that this form of training has this desirable effect."[74] That same literature review found "evidence that de-escalation trained wards increased staff risk of exposure to being involved in an aggressive incident when compared with control and restraint trained wards,"[75] highlighting the very real possibility that using force to restrain subjects earlier in an encounter may actually prevent the situation from devolving to a more dangerous point.

A 2019 review of the literature on the effectiveness of police crisis intervention training (CIT) programs published in the *Journal of the American Academy of Psychiatry and the Law* concluded that "There is little evidence in the peer-reviewed literature . . . that shows CIT's benefits on objective measures of arrests, officer injury, citizen injury, or use of force."[76] Another literature review of de-escalation training—which goes beyond CIT—concluded in a 2020 issue of *Criminology and Public Policy* that "conclusions concerning the effectiveness of de-escalation training" in the studies reviewed were "limited by the questionable quality of almost all evaluation research designs."[77]

Despite a dearth of evidence that provides strong support for the idea that more de-escalation training would significantly reduce police uses of force, it may still be possible that continuing to invest in de-escalation training could have some moderate but nevertheless positive effects on at least some relevant outcomes. We just have to go into such efforts with our eyes wide open to the limits of such a policy program.

One of those limits is the extremely short and chaotic time frames within which so many police shootings and other uses of force occur. Consider a 2018 officer-involved shooting in Los Angeles that began with a noise complaint regarding a "screaming woman." That shooting was captured on video, which begins with the responding officers knocking on the door from behind which the noise was coming. The officers were quickly met by a completely naked man wielding a large knife, who rushed one of the officers within seven seconds of the door opening, which was just 45 seconds after the officers knocked.[78] De-escalation techniques take time to implement; and in many (though not all) cases, officers don't have that luxury.

While there remain many questions about the effectiveness of de-escalation training for police, some new experiments have shown promise, highlighting the value of continued exploration in this space.

## CONCLUSION

I think the widespread anger and frustration expressed across the country in the wake of George Floyd's murder has two main sources. One is an overestimation of the scope of the problem of excessive police force. Hopefully, this chapter has given you a better sense of what the data do and don't support in the way of characterizations of how police fall short in their duty to exercise restraint. The other source of the frustration, I think, is the belief that there are ready solutions to the problems that do exist in policing. As understandable as the desire for clear answers to serious questions is, this belief is as misplaced as the assertion that policing is a fundamentally rotten enterprise. The reality is far more complicated and requires more nuance than many bring with them to discussions of these issues—something even I need to be reminded of every now and then.

Not only is police use of force a much rarer phenomenon than the tenor of our public discourse might suggest, some of the most popular ideas to address it don't actually seem likely to fix the problem, to the extent we have one. In some cases, those proposals might even make things worse. Still, there are things we can do to make policing better. This chapter mentions a few of them, and I've proposed other reforms elsewhere.

If there's one thing I hope you've taken away from this chapter, it's this: The road to productive reform begins not with a rush forward, but with a step back—one that allows us to soberly consider the complicated realities that our passions may be obscuring.

# CHAPTER SIX

# THE OTHER SIDE OF THE "FALSE-POSITIVE PROBLEM"

One weekend afternoon when I was about 17 years old, a few friends and I were walking down one of the corridors at Roosevelt Field Mall in Long Island, New York. There were maybe five or six of us in the mall that day. At one point, a group of four or five white kids were walking past us in the same corridor. We looked straight into their eyes, which quickly darted away as they became silent. No one said anything, but once we'd gotten about 50 feet between us, we all laughed about how scared they were of our little crew, and we enjoyed the feeling.

You see, back then we tended to carry ourselves with attitude, so to speak—the same attitude that undergirded the explicit gangster rap we'd blast from our car stereos in the school parking lot just to piss off the teachers. We were all brown-skinned Latinos, and while most of the kids we went to school with (and most of the kids in the mall that day) wore fitted Hollister or Abercrombie & Fitch, we wore oversized Rocawear and Enyce. We also wore durags and flat-billed baseball caps (aka "fitteds"). Despite our fresh fades or well-kempt cornrows, we didn't look "clean-cut," and despite the fact that we (most of us, anyway) were good kids below the surface, we preferred it that way.

While we didn't expect the rich kids from Manhasset or Garden City to test us in the middle of a mall, there was always the chance of running into actual gang members from Hempstead or Freeport who just might. So the utility of our little tough-guy act extended beyond a few chuckles at the expense of some corny-looking "rich" kids. If we showed we were willing to fight (and, foolishly, we were), it was much less likely we'd be messed with by those we really didn't want to have a problem with.

Not long after that day at the mall, I walked into my local deli for a bacon, egg, and cheese sandwich. I had on my usual clothes and had music blasting from my headphones. There was an older white woman in line in front of me who turned around. Like those kids at the mall, she averted her eyes from mine. She also—discreetly—took her purse off her shoulder and clutched it in front of her. Now, the thought of snatching someone's purse had never crossed my mind. But she was a stranger and couldn't have known I was a good kid. Neither could she have known otherwise. So why the suspicion? It had to be the picture before her that gave her the idea that I might be a threat—the same picture that my friends and I were happy to paint at the mall. This time, though, the effect wasn't funny. I realized that what I was putting out into the world through the way I dressed, spoke, and walked and the look on my face—all of it was sending a message that was likely going to cost me way more than it would ever get me.

So how are two 20-year-old stories relevant to modern debates about policing and criminal justice? The answer is that they illustrate a reality that might help us better understand the dynamics of the false-positive problem—a term that describes police stopping, engaging with, or detaining people pursuant to suspicions that turn out to be nothing more than that.

In a thoughtful and expertly argued essay on this topic, my Manhattan Institute colleague and mentor James Copland urged readers "to think carefully about this false-positive problem."[1] And we should, because, as Columbia University's John McWhorter put it in his 2003 book, *Authentically Black*, "racial profiling is not just one problem on the landscape of race relations—it is the main thing distracting African-Americans from sensing themselves as true Americans rather than a 'people apart.'"[2]

## FALSE POSITIVES AND THE CODE OF THE STREET

The false-positive problem, and what it's thought to represent, has animated much of the antipathy expressed toward the institution of policing; it has inspired litigation, investigations, and reforms aimed at limiting police activity—particularly in minority neighborhoods.

On a webpage titled "Ending Racist Stop and Frisk," the Massachusetts chapter of the ACLU notes in a section of "key facts" that more than 200,000 of the police-civilian encounters initiated by Boston police "led to no arrest," and that "only 2.5% led to seizure of contraband."[3] Similar statistics were cited by those prosecuting the case against the NYPD's stop-and-frisk practices during this century's first decade. In an article purporting to prove that the criminal justice system is racist, the *Washington Post's* Radley Balko cites a study finding that Black motorists were more likely than white motorists to be searched when stopped by police even though "whites were more likely to be found with illicit drugs."[4]

Being on the civilian side of a police encounter that turns out to be a false positive—that is, the encounter does not reveal evidence of a crime—can be both infuriating and deeply embarrassing. You can multiply those emotions by 10 when such encounters involve Black and brown men, which have been the subject of incredibly contentious debates about race and policing. The false-positive problem is perhaps the main contributor to the cloud of racial tension that hangs over many police interactions, because whenever a Black or brown male is stopped and frisked without the police finding any contraband, it contributes to the sense—widely held in many sectors of American society—that the typical police officer, through his subscription to negative stereotypes and his own biases, views people of color as criminals. Right or wrong, such encounters are regularly seized on to make the case that policing is an institution imbued with racism.

In his book *Code of the Street*—an ethnographic work (and one of the most important contributions to the sociological literature in my lifetime) that informs much of what's to come in this chapter—sociologist Elijah Anderson describes the disturbing phenomenon of Black men "almost always [being] given extra scrutiny" by sales personnel when shopping in nicer neighborhoods, illustrating "the inability of some whites to make distinctions—particularly between people who are out to commit crime and those who are not."[5]

And in 2016, Republican senator Tim Scott eloquently recounted on the Senate floor his own personal stories of being stopped and questioned by police pursuant to what turned out to be baseless suspicions that left him, as it does other Black men, "feeling like you're being targeted for nothing more than being just yourself."[6]

When undergoing my own effort to think carefully about this problem, I remembered the stories at the top of this chapter and began to consider the following question: What if at least part of the false-positive problem isn't just driven by police acting on racial biases, but also by cops picking up on cues that Black and brown men are *themselves* purposefully putting out into the world—cues associated with the kind of criminality police are trying to prevent and suss out?

In both popular culture and the sociological literature, one will find evidence that suggests this may very well be the case. That is, one will find evidence that, particularly in America's urban Black neighborhoods, many people adopt and perform behaviors that, to varying degrees, outwardly communicate comfort with and proximity to violence and/or criminality.

That's not to say that every false positive is the fault of the person stopped. Nor is it to say that those involved in such encounters somehow deserved to endure those experiences. But whether false positives should always be considered evidence of racial bias on the part of police would seem a key question in contemporary debates about criminal justice reform. As such, we ought to consider evidence that might suggest that the answer to that question is no. What follows is an attempt to marshal some of that evidence.


IN 1978, RICHARD PRYOR opened his *Live in Concert* special with a joke about the discomfort felt by the white people rushing back from intermission to find that their seats had been commandeered by Black audience members. He went on to note how nice white people get when they're around a lot of Black people. Pryor comedically contrasted that niceness with how Black people "gorilla their way in the place," cutting the line while saying things like "move out the way, mothafucka," leaving dead white people in their wake.[7] The crowd roared with laughter, recognizing the many kernels of truth undergirding the bit.

A little more than 20 years later, Cedric the Entertainer would expound on the same phenomenon in *The Original Kings of Comedy*, explaining that while white people might "hope" no one takes their seats in the event they're running late to a show, Black people, by contrast, live by a "more confrontational" creed in that they'd "wish a mothafucka would" be in their seats.[8]

That contrast formed the premise of a 1991 episode of *The Fresh Prince of Bel-Air*. In the episode, Carlton Banks—a tightly wound, snobbish, Black teenager raised by a wealthy family in a Bel-Air mansion who was often teased for behaving and dressing like a white guy, or a "sellout"[9]—takes a bet that he can withstand 72 hours navigating the tough Los Angeles suburb of Compton.[10] Over the course of the episode, Carlton eventually proves he can fit in, shedding his khakis and cable-knit cardigans (as well as the queen's English), adopting Ebonics, and donning flashy, oversized clothes accentuated by gaudy jewelry. He even went on to take the street name "C-Note," ultimately blurring, to the audience's surprise and amusement, the once-stark difference between him and the gangster types he agrees to spend the weekend with.

These comedic pieces were all based on the idea that the aggressive, quasi-criminal postures they described are an element of Black urban identity. That idea is ever present in much of modern hip-hop. Brooklyn rapper Joell Ortiz (whose music I truly enjoy) proudly describes in his song "Hip-Hop" the posture of someone staying true to the East Coast hip-hop culture:

The good ol' two-step, the classic head-nod
The thirsty ice-grill [slang for a dirty look or the face
   of someone thirsty for a fight], who wants to get
   robbed? . . .
This is hip-hop

In many of America's Black and brown neighborhoods lots of young men carry themselves in a way that communicates their "realness"—that is, their toughness, as well as their distrust and dislike of law enforcement.

Consider the song "R.N.S." (short for "Real N**** Shit") by the rap group Slaughterhouse, which counts never taking the stand (that is, snitching) on someone among the elements of realness.[11] The song's music video closes by depicting a police officer being overpowered, disarmed, and chased down by thugs. The antisocial elements of street realness are the objects of an incisive critique in rapper J. Cole's "Ville Mentality," which describes the misguided but widely adopted attitudes as a series of declarations:

N**** play [fool, embarrass, take advantage of] me—Never!
Give up my chain—Never! . . .
Show 'em my pain—Never!
Dirt on my name—Never!

The tough-guy posture described in these songs is something you'd actually see on a Friday night stroll through the streets of Brownsville, Brooklyn, or Manhattan's Washington Heights. But you wouldn't only see it on the faces of the local drug dealers or stick-up kids. You'd also see some of those same vibes brought to life on the faces and in the appearances of good, law-abiding kids on their way home from school.

This is something that Elijah Anderson so expertly documented in his renowned 1999 work *Code of the Street: Decency, Violence, and the Moral Life of the Inner City*:

> Many of the black middle-class youths use the street as a place to gather and talk with their friends, and they adopt the clothing styles of the poorer people farther down the avenue. So people who are not familiar with black people are sometimes unable to distinguish between who is law-abiding and who is not. The resulting confusion appears to be a standing problem for the police and local store owners, and it may lead to a sense of defensiveness among middle-class residents who fear being violated or robbed. *But promising protection on the street, it is a confusion that many youths seem not to mind and at times work to encourage.*[12] (emphasis added)

That passage brings to mind Dave Chappelle's 2017 Netflix comedy special, *Equanimity*, in which he sheepishly acknowledged that, contrary to what he called a "popular misconception," he was not, in fact, "from the hood."[13] He went on, "But I never bothered to correct anybody because I wanted the streets to embrace me . . . As a matter of fact, I kept it up as a ruse." In other words, there were certain benefits that would attend Chappelle's association with "hood" street culture.

What Chappelle had done throughout his career was what Anderson referred to as "profiling"—a term he defined as people "'representing' the image of themselves by which they would like to be known: who they are and how they stand in relation to whom." As an example, he described the mostly Black students at Germantown High School, some of whom, despite not being part of "the street element," nonetheless had "a need to show themselves as being capable of dealing with the street."[14] Why might that be? Anderson convincingly concluded that an informal "code" or set of rules of behavior that predominates in many inner city communities—one that places a premium on "[p]ossession of respect" and "the credible threat of vengeance"— induces even the law-abiding toward repeated public displays of their own "nerve and heart" in order to "build a reputation . . . that works to deter aggression and disrespect, which are sources of great anxiety on the inner-city street."[15]

On his 2021 album, *The Off-Season*, J. Cole recalled in a moment of honest introspection that in addition to fearing the sort of violent death that had befallen others in his neighbor-hood, he also feared being physically dominated in the presence of others—something my friends and I referred to as "getting punked" during my teenage years. One way to stave this off is precisely what Cole describes in a song entitled "Let Go My Hand," during which he admits to "pretending" by keeping "a tough demeanor on the surface." While this "bluff" worked "way more often than not," Cole says over a jazzy beat, eventually, he'd be forced to fight in order to "save face."

Anderson's volume contains a number of vivid descriptions and illustrations of such public displays:

> "On certain street corners or down certain alleys, groups
> of boys . . . profile or represent, striking stylized poses,
> almost always dressed in expensive clothes that belie their

unemployed status. They lead others to the easy conclusion that they 'clock' (work) in the drug trade."[16]

Other scholars have documented the same phenomenon and studied its effects. Some examples: In 1995, Columbia University's Trey Ellis confessed in *Speak My Name: Black Men on Black Masculinity and the American Dream*[17] that he and his friends would "sometimes take perverse pride in the fear the combination of our sex and skin instills in everyone else." A 2005 paper by criminologist Charis E. Kubrin in *Social Problems*, titled "Gangstas, Thugs, and Hustlas: Identity and the Code of the Street in Rap Music," documents the presence of the code of the street in hip-hop. And a 2010 study published in *Criminology* found that "Consistent with Anderson's hypotheses, neighborhood street culture significantly predicts violent delinquency," particularly "in neighborhoods where the street culture is endorsed widely."[18]

While the sorts of outward-facing displays described by Anderson can work as deterrents, they can also invite unwanted attention—not just from police, but also from gang members that are actually looking for trouble. In an interview published by *Complex* magazine, the late rapper Nipsey Hussle (who was shot and killed in 2019) described the kinds of gang warfare he engaged in: "As a gang banger, when you go on a mission, when you're looking for your so-called enemy [ . . .] you're gonna pass up a dude who's dressed square. You're gonna pass up a dude from a different race, but when you see someone that's dressed like you dress, got the walk that you got, and got the body language like you, you're gonna say, 'There you go. Get him.' And that's deep [ . . .]. You're looking for yourself on the other side of town, and you're gonna hop out and try to attack him."

The study of how people alter their own behavior in order to inform others' impressions of them has a long pedigree in the modern sociological literature. In his seminal 1956 work *The Presentation of Self in Everyday Life*, Canadian sociologist Erving Goffman laid out the two primary kinds of communication—"expressions given and expressions given off."[19] While it is certainly possible—indeed common—for people to give off impressions they didn't mean to, Goffman made a compelling case that people "will intentionally and consciously express [themselves] in a particular way, but chiefly because the tradition of his group or social status require this kind of expression."[20] As an example, Goffman quoted sociologist Willard Waller, who found that in college dormitories, "a girl who is called to the telephone . . . will often allow herself to be called several times, in order to give all the other girls ample opportunity to hear her paged."[21] He also cited an interview given by a teacher who discussed putting on a tough façade to induce fear in her students in order to deter them from misbehaving.

In Goffman's view, we are all playing roles in the play of life, and society is our stage. Some of us will get so deep into character that there ceases to be a distinction between our persona and who we really are, as the former bleeds further and further into the latter. But there is a moral element to this state of affairs. According to Goffman, "Society is organized on the principle that . . . an individual who implicitly or explicitly signifies that he has certain social characteristics ought in fact to be what he claims he is."[22] Through the signals one gives and gives off, he says, one "implicitly forgoes all claims to be things he does not appear to be and hence forgoes the treatment that would be appropriate for such individuals."[23]

If Goffman is right about this idea, that people are what they project, undergirding our societal structure, then we begin to see how it might be difficult for some—even police—to overcome the default setting of reading our signals as truthful.

If something as innocuous as standing or walking a certain way while wearing certain kinds of clothes can easily (according to Anderson) lead one to surmise that a group of inner-city boys are involved in criminal activity, one can imagine how police may sometimes fail to distinguish between those who are "representing" because they actually are involved in street life and those "representing" because they prefer to be seen that way for the sake of looking cool, fitting in, or deterring unwanted aggression. The resulting confusion constitutes an ongoing problem that has strained police–community relations in American cities for decades.

This leaves us with a question of what to do about that problem. I agree with McWhorter, who recognized that "refrain[ing] from focusing on young black men who exhibit clusters of traits and behaviors that reasonably suggest involvement in the drug trade," or other crimes for that matter, would "leav[e] innocent residents of poor neighborhoods at the mercy of hardened criminals."[24] The solution, McWhorter wrote, depends on "whether we can 'profile' intelligently, in a way that does not leave black America feeling persecuted by marauding gangs of white men with guns."

That's a question that doesn't seem to have a clear answer, but the key here is to understand that, to the extent false positives contribute to that sense of persecution, reconsidering the amount of blame we should place on police as the main drivers of false positives could help soften the hardened sense of mistrust of police in America's inner cities. How? By raising genuine questions about whether and to what extent police conduct is a reasonable reaction to behaviors and attitudes calculated to communicate comfort with and proximity to (if not involvement in) violence and other criminal activity. In other words, the complex realities that undergird the behaviors of those in minority neighborhoods where the code prevails should perhaps temper critiques of police based on the prevalence of false positives in minority neighborhoods.

That said, even if false positives are, in significant part, a function of people acting out the code of the street, police (like any group of people) still have biases that they may or may not act on. And that's a real problem. Some of those biases may be a function of the brain's tendency to recognize patterns, which lead people to rely on heuristics that function as mental shortcuts when processing complex information. Whatever its cause, however, reducing bias is a mission we ought to get behind as a society.

Interesting empirical work has been done to assess whether certain types of trainings and field experiences reduce bias on the part of police officers making decisions about whether to use deadly force.[25] Some of that research suggests that some officers may be able to learn to override the biases thought to inform racial disparities in their decisions to shoot or not to shoot suspects in simulated training modules; however, that research also seems to show that the modest benefits of such trainings and experiences as seen in laboratory environments may not manifest themselves when officers are actually making those decisions in the field under less ideal conditions (for example, when they are fatigued, frightened, or stressed).

A more important thread in that research shows that the benefits of certain kinds of anti-bias training are unlikely to override the impact of real-world experience when that experience aligns with certain stereotypes. Indeed, one study found that "the capacity of an officer's training and experience to reduce bias may depend heavily on the degree to which the environment reinforces the stereotype that Blacks are dangerous."[26] Interestingly, however, the officers who were most likely to work in stereotype-congruent environments (and therefore least likely to show less bias in response to training) nonetheless outperformed civilian community members in weapon detection and set more conservative criteria for the decision to shoot.

The decision to shoot is the most extreme context in which we might see a false positive. And though rare, instances of police mistaking a cell phone for a gun are incredibly tragic and understandably infuriating to those in communities that have come to see police as racially biased actors.

In more routine, lower-stakes interactions, however, what we know seems to suggest that the behavior of community members in public spaces could be a significant contributor to officers' decision-making, as well as to their own preconceived notions. One finds support for this theory in a controversial study by Harvard economist Roland Fryer, who did not find evidence of racial bias in police shootings but did find it in the data on lower levels of force, like shoving.[27]

Citizens' behavior is also a significant contributor to how police deploy their resources, which leads us to another argument that should frame how we think about the false-positive problem.

## THE ROLE OF CRIME PATTERNS

Since at least the time the late, great Jack Maple started putting pins on a map to identify geographic patterns in New York City's street crime, police have been deploying their officers to the areas that need the most attention. As noted in chapter 1, the reality of crime in the United States—particularly violent crime—is that it is both geographically and demographically concentrated. That concentration informs how police departments deploy their officers, which, in turn, impacts the data on various measures ranging from traffic stops to arrests and searches.

As tempting as it may be to rely on racial disparities in false-positive encounters to conclude that policing is an endeavor animated by racial bias, we have to remember the following statistical reality: Who police encounter is very much a function of where police spend their time. So, if police departments are deploying a disproportionate percentage of their officers to certain neighborhoods based on crime trends, that's where a disproportionate percentage of police mistakes are going to happen.

Whatever the data point in question, we can't simply view racial disparities in a vacuum. Just as disproportionately high rates of incarceration among men are a function of the fact that men commit violent crime at disproportionately higher rates than women, the fact that a disproportionate number of false positives seem to involve Black and brown men is at least partly a function of the larger police presence in Black and brown communities, which, in turn is largely a function of crime rates.

For an illustration, consider a paper published by the New York Civil Liberties Union (NYCLU) in 2019, which criticizes the NYPD's practices of stopping, questioning, and, in some cases, frisking individuals during the first half of Mayor Bill de Blasio's administration (2014–2017).[28] The report focuses heavily on both the disproportionate representation of Black and Latino people among those stopped, questioned, and frisked, as well as on the number of false positives, which are referred to as "innocent stops."

According to the report, Black and Latino people were the subjects of "four [80 percent] of every five reported stops." But crime trends in New York City precincts during the decade of 2010–2019 provide some much-needed context for those interested in an accurate interpretation of the data presented by the NYCLU.[29] Those trends show that stop activity is concentrated in precincts with significantly higher numbers and rates of crime.

Between 2010 and 2019, the 15 precincts the NYCLU identified (which house an estimated 1,701,957 residents)[30] as having the most reported stops (excluding the borough of Staten Island) saw:

- 251,264 (25 percent) of the seven major felonies recorded by the NYPD in the Bronx, Brooklyn, Manhattan, and Queens (excluding the Central Park precinct)[31]—an average annual rate of 1,476.3 per 100,000.

- 1,276 (36 percent) of the homicides in those four boroughs[32]—an average annual rate of 7.5 per 100,000.

- 165,518 (31 percent) of the seven nonmajor felonies tracked by the NYPD in those boroughs[33]—an average annual rate of 972.5 per 100,000.

- 22,368 (47 percent) of the dangerous weapons offenses[34]— an average annual rate of 131.4 per 100,000.

By contrast, the 15 precincts[35] identified by the NYCLU (which house an estimated 1,265,913 residents)[36] as having the fewest reported stops (again, excluding Staten Island and Central Park) saw significantly lower crime rates than those above—particularly regarding homicides and dangerous weapons offenses. These precincts accounted for just

- 167,096 (17 percent) of the seven major felonies recorded by the NYPD in the Bronx, Brooklyn, Manhattan, and Queens between 2010 and 2019[37]—an average annual rate of 1,320.0 per 100,000.

- 225 (6 percent) of the homicides in those four boroughs[38]—an average annual rate of 1.8 per 100,000.

- 52,547 (10 percent) of the seven nonmajor felonies tracked by the NYPD in those boroughs[39]—an average annual rate of 415.1 per 100,000.

- 3,548 (7 percent) of the dangerous weapons offenses[40]—an average annual rate of 28.0 per 100,000.

The above numbers lend support to the claim that stop activity is a function of where the crime happens. And consistent with the idea that police are going to have more opportunities for false positives in the places they spend more of their time, 11 of the precincts identified by the NYCLU as among the 15 with the most stop activity (again, excluding Staten Island) were also among the 15 precincts identified as having the highest number of "innocent stops." As for the NYCLU's focus on the disproportionate representation of Black and Hispanic people among those stopped by the NYPD, one should consider Black and

Hispanic overrepresentation among violent crime victims and perpetrators. According to the NYPD's Supplementary Homicide Reports,[41] between 2016 and 2019, Black and Hispanic people constituted 1,057 (86.2 percent) of the 1,226 homicide victims whose race/ethnicity were known to the NYPD, and 795 (89.7 percent) of the 886 homicide perpetrators whose race/ethnicity were known by the NYPD.

It's also worth noting that every last one of the 15 precincts with the *most* stop activity (which, as noted above, had significantly more crime than those with the least stop activity) was among the 15 precincts identified by the NYCLU as having the most reported stops of Black and Latino people, and 14 of the 15 precincts with the *least* stop activity (which, as noted above, had significantly less crime than those with the most activity) were among the 15 precincts identified by the NYCLU report as having the fewest stops of Black and Latino people.[42]

Reinforcing the idea that the deployment of police resources is driven by serious violent crime are data published by the Chicago Police Department in its 2020 annual report, regarding the geographic concentration of shootings, homicides, carjackings, calls for service, investigatory stops, and gun recoveries. The report includes heat maps (see figure 3) showing the locations of the city's homicides, non-fatal shootings, and gun recoveries (64 percent of which involved an arrest).[43] Notice how similar the first two maps look to the map of gun recoveries (see figure 4).

What's really interesting is that if you look at the top five Chicago police districts (that is, precincts) for the categories of carjackings, non-fatal shootings, homicides, and calls for service, only nine of the city's 22 police districts are represented on those

**Figure 3.** *Source: 2020 Chicago Police Department Annual Report*

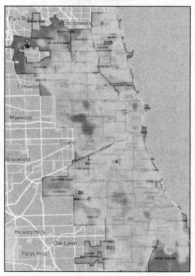

**Figure 4.** *Source: 2020 Chicago Police Department Annual Report*

four lists—the 3rd, 4th, 6th, 7th, 8th, 10th, 11th, 15th, and 25th. Look at the top five districts for investigatory stops (see Table 3), and you'll see that there is only one that did not also appear among the top five of the five categories just mentioned (the 9th, which was at the bottom of the list and was by no means a low-crime part of the city).

### TABLE 3

**Top-Five Police Districts: Investigatory Stop Reports (2020)**

| Police District | Number of Stops | Other Top-Five List Appearances (place on list) |
|---|---|---|
| 7th | 10,137 | • Non-Fatal Shootings (2nd) |
| | | • Homicides (3rd) |
| | | • Firearm Recoveries (2nd) |
| 11th | 7,706 | • Non-Fatal Shootings (1st) |
| | | • Homicides (1st) |
| | | • Carjackings (1st) |
| | | • Firearm Recoveries (1st) |
| | | • Calls for Service (1st) |
| 25th* | 6,281 | • Calls for Service |
| 8th† | 6,028 | • Calls for Service |
| 9th‡ | 5,446 | N/A |

Source: 2020 Chicago Police Department annual report

\* Shares its southern border with the 11th and 15th districts, which are among the city's most dangerous
† Shares its eastern border with the 7th (which appears in second and third place, respectively on the lists for non-fatal shootings and homicides)
‡ Shares its southern border with the 7th

The fact of the matter is that—no matter which way you slice things—we'll never fully understand the statistics on the racial breakdowns of police activity until we acknowledge that these statistics are at least partly a function of racially disparate crime trends, and other social phenomena.

## THE PROBLEM WITH NYC'S STOP-AND-FRISK DATA

"Stop and frisk," or, more accurately, "stop, *question*, and *sometimes* frisk," is one of those odd phrases to which many attribute a certain meaning without being exactly sure just what that meaning is. In a technical sense, you could make the case for the phrase merely referring to a police power recognized by the US Supreme Court more than 50 years ago in a case called *Terry v. Ohio*,[44] which remains good law today. The central holding of that case can be fairly summarized as follows.

The Constitution's Fourth Amendment does not require police to delay taking investigative action until after a crime has been committed, and such actions can include stopping, questioning, and, in some cases, frisking individuals on the basis of reasonable suspicion (as opposed to probable cause—the standard police must meet to make an arrest or conduct a more intrusive search, say, of someone's home) that the individual has committed or is about to commit a crime. Frisking is allowed only when there is reasonable suspicion to believe that the person is armed and might pose a danger to the officer(s) conducting the investigation.

Especially in New York City, "*Terry* stops," as they're called, have been broadly maligned by police critics and reform advocates as both ineffective crime-fighting tools and as a means for the oppression of Black and brown communities. However, both assertions are based on an unjustifiable confidence in the soundness of an inherently flawed dataset.

The mid-1990s marked the beginning of a sharp upward trend in the number of *Terry* stops reported by NYPD officers. One driver of this was a function of the department reorienting itself around the idea that its officers should be preventing crime and not just responding to it. One way to do that was to keep an eye out for suspicious behavior that might lead to the discovery of contraband or an open warrant. Another driver, according to the department's detractors and officers alike, was that the department's leadership created an incentive structure that placed informal pressure on officers to show their proactivity through the generation of stop reports known as UF-250s, or 250s for short.

The annual growth in the number of 250s filed was happening during a period of sharply declining crime, which gave defenders of the NYPD's stop practices a good piece of ammunition to use against those attacking the practice on the grounds that it was used disproportionately against Black and brown men. These were indeed the competing claims when the NYPD was sued in federal court by a class of plaintiffs who alleged the department's stop practices violated the Fourth and Fourteenth Amendments' clauses regarding unreasonable searches and equal protection.[45] The lead plaintiff was a man named David Floyd.[46]

A district court judge ruled against the NYPD, which appealed the ruling up to the Second Circuit Court of Appeals, but the election of Bill de Blasio as the 109th mayor of New York City put an end to that. Mayor de Blasio campaigned against stop and frisk, so it was not a surprise when dropping the city's appeal was one of his first acts as mayor.[47] The case was settled by the city, and part of the court-approved settlement imposed a corporate monitor to oversee the department's future compliance with a host of reforms to which the city had committed.

The district court ruling largely mirrored the critiques leveled against the NYPD by complaining activists. In short, the judge held that there was inadequate justification for the sharp growth in reported stops and that the disproportionate effect of that growth on minority communities was sufficient evidence of unconstitutionally discriminatory policing.[48] The court's ruling was based in part on the idea that unjustifiable stops were a function of an unofficial quota of sorts—that downward pressure applied by supervisors and commanders, coupled with the inclusion of stop activity as a performance measure in departmental reviews, created an incentive structure that encouraged officers to report as much stop activity as they could. Based on conversations I've had with NYPD service members that were in patrol-type roles during the first decade of the 2000s, there is certainly a good bit of truth in the incentivization point.

In the two years that followed the ruling, the number of stops reported by NYPD officers declined sharply, going from more than 680,000 in 2011 down to about 12,000 in 2016, all while crime continued to decline. In 2017, New York City would see its lowest modern-era murder tally. Critics on both the left and right seized on these simultaneous trends as definitive proof that the NYPD had been lying all along—that is, that the practice was not central to the city's victory over crime and could be discarded without consequence. This is a fair point to raise, but the strength of this argument depends on the veracity and reliability of the numbers on which it's based. There are at least three reasons to believe that the trendline in actual versus reported *Terry* stops was flatter than the high- and low-end numbers indicate.

The first of these is the legal complexity of police–civilian interactions. In New York City, there are four levels of police encounters. These levels, set out in a 1976 appellate court case called *People v. DeBour*, are (1) request for information, (2) common law right of inquiry, (3) *Terry* stop, and (4) arrest. The first thing to know here is that during a level 1 or 2 encounter, the individual with whom the officer is interacting is *not* being detained and is free to terminate the interaction at any time. The second thing to know is that the lines between the first three of these levels are not always clear.

The intricacies of what makes an interaction a level 1, 2, or 3 encounter are detailed in a publicly available document approved by the NYPD's corporate monitor and distributed by the department at its Command Level Training Conference in September 2015 titled "Investigative Encounters Reference Guide." That document spends more than 20 pages outlining the complex legal distinctions between each level—distinctions whose application veteran prosecutors, defense attorneys, and judges regularly disagree about. As such, it is more than understandable for cops—the vast majority of whom are not trained lawyers—to make errors when applying these standards in the field without the benefit of paralegals or legal research assistants to run questions by. So why base an analysis of stops on the assumption that cops never incorrectly logged a level 1 or 2 interaction as a level 3 encounter—particularly given the incentive argument critics made?

The difficulties of distinguishing between the levels of encounters were likely exacerbated by another reality: Many, if not most, civilians didn't have a particularly firm grasp of their right to terminate certain interactions with the police. This reality is what undergirded the city council's 2017 passage of the Right to Know Act,[49] which requires officers to, among other things, affirmatively apprise civilians of their right to refuse search requests in the absence of probable cause. This act was based on the city council's explicit finding that "many New Yorkers are unaware of their constitutional rights when interacting with law enforcement officers,"[50] and it constitutes the second reason to be skeptical of the stop data relied upon to make the case against the NYPD's stop practices.

Prior to the enactment of this law, NYPD officers were sometimes able to avail themselves of a civilian's mistaken belief that he could not refuse consent to a search. The Supreme Court had drawn clear lines as to such searches. In *Florida v. Bostick*,[51] for example, the court held that "when officers have no basis for suspecting a particular individual, they may generally ask questions of that individual, ask to examine the individual's identification, and request consent to search his or her luggage [or person, backpack, etc.], *as long as the police do not convey a message that compliance with their requests is required*" (emphasis added). The court had never held that, in order to avoid conveying "a message that compliance with their requests is required," the police must go out of their way to inform someone of his or her rights. Indeed, the court had expressly rejected—as it did in *U.S. v. Drayton*[52]—the notion that police must inform citizens of their right to refuse searches, observing that nothing in its cases "suggest[s] that . . . a presumption of invalidity attaches [to a search] if a citizen consented without explicit notification that he or she was free to refuse to cooperate."

That calls for a law making it more difficult for police to acquire consent for searches came so soon after a legal victory that resulted in such a sharp decline in reported *Terry* stops indicates that at least some of the interactions that might previously have been reported as stops were now being (perhaps rightly) categorized as consensual interactions during which individuals were technically free to go.

This takes me to the third reason for skepticism of the stop data: The corporate monitor's finding of widespread underreporting of stops by NYPD officers.

As I mentioned earlier, the settlement of the stop-and-frisk litigation meant that the NYPD would be overseen by a corporate monitor. That monitor, Peter L. Zimroth, would file regular reports with the Southern District Court of New York. In the report filed on December 13, 2017, Zimroth detailed what was described as an "issue of underreporting" *Terry* stops, telling the court that "Some officers making stops do not file the required stop forms documenting them, in part because of what appears to be an exaggerated fear of discipline and lawsuits."[53]

According to an audit led by the department's Quality Assurance Division (QAD), the underreporting issue was significant in its size and scope. As part of the audit detailed in the December 2017 report, the QAD identified 50 arrests—for criminal possession of a controlled substance or weapons—effected across the city that stemmed from a stop that should have been documented. In just 13 of those cases was there a corresponding stop report on file.[54] The QAD also looked at 46 arrests for criminal trespass in New York City Housing Authority (NYCHA) buildings that stemmed from stops officers were required to document. But only 17 of them were.[55]

What's interesting particularly given the points regarding legal complexity—is that the number of arrests initially identified by the QAD for these two audits was 154 for the drug and weapon possession arrests and 62 for the NYCHA trespass arrests. Those numbers were revised downward to 50 and 46 after further investigation.

So here's what we know: (1) Due to perceived risk of discipline, NYPD officers underreported stops following the conclusion of the *Floyd* litigation; (2) reform advocates pressured the city council to pass the Right to Know Act in part because individuals were still being searched pursuant to consent they didn't know they could withhold; and (3) the legal distinctions between the sorts of interactions that must be reported and those that do not have to be reported are complex and subject to human error.

Given all that, what I'd like for you to consider is this: Isn't it likely that, when the incentive structure encouraged stop reports, officers *overreported* stops by, among other things (like fabricating 250s), erroneously (if not purposefully) reporting level 1 and 2 interactions as level 3 stops, and that this overreporting artificially inflated the number of *Terry* stops allegedly conducted by the NYPD? If the answer is yes, then a large grain of salt should accompany the arguments based on those numbers.

## CONCLUSION

Buttressed by empirical analyses and crime data, there seems to be a concretely identifiable "code of the street" that informs both the behaviors adopted by those in inner-city neighborhoods and the perceptions of police trying to suss out and prevent crime. Those behaviors can sometimes lead police to misperceive situations, resulting in false-positive encounters, which in turn feed the sense that minorities are often singled out for unfair treatment by racially biased police. That sense is further fed by the role that crime trends play in police resource deployment, which can result in a higher concentration of false positives among minority residents of higher-crime neighborhoods. Moreover, the scope of the false-positive problem is also one that, at least in New York City, may be overstated by the data on stops, which may not be as reliable as was once thought.

Despite the contextualizing research and data outlined in the sections above, police critics have nevertheless seized on the false-positive problem to push a host of reforms, lawsuits, and investigations calculated to reduce police proactivity. The impact of these efforts can sometimes be hard to concretely identify, but the information we do have disturbingly points us to the conclusion that the collective impact of these efforts has been to make many city streets less safe—an impact that has fallen disproportionately on the shoulders of the very people in whose names the reforms, lawsuits, and investigations were pursued.

# CHAPTER SEVEN

# RACE: THE ELEPHANT IN THE ROOM

During a discussion about the systemic racism debate with a Black police officer who, at the time, was working in one of the most dangerous precincts in the country, he said something that stuck with me for years. He said—and I'm paraphrasing, since it's been awhile:

"A truly racist cop isn't the guy constantly getting out of his car, frisking people, and clearing corners to try and prevent shit from happening. A truly racist cop is the guy that says, 'Fuck 'em. Let 'em kill each other.' But the haters want us to act more like the racist and less like the go-getter. So, what does that say about them?"

AS WITH ALL HUMAN endeavors, activities, and institutions, one would not have to look long at America's criminal justice system to find disparities along all manner of lines—age, gender, ethnicity, and, yes, race. The latter of these constitutes a central point of contention in debates about American criminal justice. In the aftermath of the protests that swept so many of the nation's streets and institutions after the deaths of Michael Brown and Eric Garner in 2014, the Black Lives Matter movement and its supporters have seized on disparities in criminal enforcement measures from arrests and stops to sentences and police uses of force, and they've done so to make the case that "systemic racism" has rigged American criminal justice against Black and Latino people.

## THE DISTINCTION BETWEEN UNEQUAL AND INEQUITABLE

There are no shortages of racial disparities in the criminal justice data. I'm sure you've heard most of them, but examples include:

- "White people make up roughly 62 percent of the U.S. population but only about 49 percent of those who are killed by police officers. African Americans, however, account for 24 percent of those fatally shot and killed by the police despite being just 13 percent of the U.S. population."[1]

- "African-American adults are 5.9 times as likely to be incarcerated than whites and Hispanics are 3.1 times as likely."[2]

- "Blacks were 3.7 times more likely to be arrested for marijuana possession than whites in 2010, even though their rate of marijuana usage was comparable."[3]

The thing to keep in mind is that what these facts—and they are, indeed, facts—say about the criminal justice system is not self-evident. As the philosopher John Stuart Mill wrote in his classic essay *On Liberty*, "Very few facts are able to tell their own story, without comments to bring about their meaning."[4] The question, then, is what conclusions can be drawn from these facts. Critics of the criminal justice system assert that disparities such as those highlighted above constitute prima facie evidence of racism within the system.

To make that assertion, however, is to play an unfair game with language, because the assertion seems to capitalize on the common understanding of a word without being constrained by that word's meaning. You see, by "systemic racism," critics are not necessarily referring to the harboring of racial animus by those working within the justice system. As those critics freely admit, "systemic racism" is a term whose definition is satisfied when systems and institutions "produce racially disparate outcomes, regardless of the intentions of the people who work within them."[5] A report summarizing research on policing published by the National Academy of Sciences (NAS) in 2018 takes pains to clarify that its use of the term "racial bias" refers "only to behavior and as used in this report is entirely agnostic as to the psychological motives or other causes that gave rise to that behavior."[6] Even referring to racial animus, the NAS report differentiates between explicit and implicit bias. The former refers to what the layperson understands an accusation of racism to mean: racist "attitudes and beliefs that are consciously endorsed by the individual" in question, whereas the latter refers to "subtle responses that are not necessarily consciously accessible to the individual and (if they are accessible) may not be endorsed."[7]

The obvious problem with this framing is that it allows critics to level a charge they can't actually support[8]—that is, as a charge of racial animus so widespread that it can characterize America's entire criminal justice system.

Distinguishing between the actual and newly contrived definitions of racism becomes more difficult in light of the ubiquity of protest movements based on the more common understanding of the term. When protesters chant "No cops. No KKK. No Racist USA!"[9] they're not talking about structures operated by people with good hearts. When an organization like Black Lives Matter talks about "state sanctioned violence and anti-Black racism," it's not talking about a faceless system that just happens to produce disparities in a way that bears no actual connection to the intent of the system's operators and designers.

The application of a term like "systemic racism" to America's criminal justice institutions implies something much more sinister than what so many of those who use the term say they really mean by it when pressed. But they know this. Their watered-down definition of racism lowers the rhetorical bar by allowing proponents of the view that criminal justice is systemically racist to sidestep the issue of intent, thereby relieving them of the burden of establishing a causal relationship between the statistical disparities latched on to in debates and the attitudes of those working within criminal justice systems. The fact is that there is no such thing as incidental racism. And if racial disparities within a particular system are not the result of racial animus, critics of that system shouldn't be allowed to get away with implying that they are.

As you'll have likely noticed by now, one of the themes of this book is that top-line criminal justice statistics can only tell you so much. Numbers, like anything else, are best understood in context. Providing context can often alter the conclusions we draw from the numbers in question. The national murder rate, for example, doesn't give one a particularly reliable sense of how dangerous a particular place is at a particular time insofar as it represents an aggregation of crimes that aren't experienced in the aggregate. The gap between incarceration rates in the US and Western Europe doesn't seem as striking once you've controlled for relevant factors like serious violent crime rates. The number of police shootings is much less jarring when viewed in light of the overall volume of police activity. And the fact that violent criminals tend to be of low socioeconomic status isn't proof of the claim that pauperism drives gun violence.

Contextualizing the racial disparities often pointed to as evidence of racism within the criminal justice system has the same effect. While such disparities are most certainly a legitimate target of intellectual inquiry, that inquiry should assess the degree to which disparities shrink once relevant, race-neutral factors are adequately controlled for. More often than not, doing so tends to limit the inferences supported by the disparities quite a bit, leaving much smaller differences that cannot obviously be explained by something other than racial animus. This was demonstrated with respect to policing in chapter 6, which illustrated how police searches of pedestrians tend to be concentrated in precincts with the highest crime levels. Indeed, searches are even more concentrated within those precincts. That concentration is going to impact the rate at which police interact with certain demographic groups if those groups are disproportionately represented in higher-crime areas. This phenomenon was noted in chapter 7 of the NAS's 2018 review of the literature on proactive policing practices, which concluded:

> Existing research demonstrates that concentrated enforcement efforts in high-crime areas and on highly active individuals can lead to racial disparities in police–citizen interactions. One consequence of this geographic concentration is observable in the geographic concentrations of arrests, SQFs, and general police activity in non-White neighborhoods in many cities. From a

statistical standpoint, this means that regression adjustment that accounts for local measured crime rates or that includes general spatial control variables . . . frequently generates findings of *substantially reduced, or even eliminated*, evidence of racial bias.[10] (emphasis added)

With respect to incarceration, another NAS report published in 2014 concluded that "racial bias and discrimination are not the primary causes of disparities in sentencing decisions or rates of imprisonment."[11] The report went on to explain:

"Overall, when statistical controls are used to take account of offense characteristics, prior criminal records, and personal characteristics, black defendants are on average sentenced *somewhat but not substantially more severely* than whites"[12] (emphasis added).

A similar assessment came from a review of the literature on sentencing disparities published at the turn of the century as part of a series of papers sponsored by the National Criminal Justice Reference Service, which concluded that while the studies that control for relevant factors "suggest that race and ethnicity do play a role—a direct role—in contemporary sentencing decisions, it would be misleading to conclude that there is a consistent and widespread pattern of direct discrimination against black and Hispanic offenders in sentencing decisions."[13]

The inclusion of adequate controls produced one of the most controversial studies on an incredibly fraught issue within the ongoing debate about race and policing—disparities in the use of deadly force by police. The study—published by Harvard economist Roland Fryer—did not find any evidence of racial bias on the part of police regarding the decision to shoot a suspect, once a host of variables were controlled for.[14] I should note again that the study *did* find significant evidence of racial bias against Black people in the use of *non*deadly force (which, as noted earlier, is still a statistically rare occurrence). But the top-line disparities decreased by 66 percent once adequate controls were incorporated into the analysis. Whether a significant portion of the remaining disparities could be attributed to unobservable factors other than animus on the part of the police officers in question is less clear, but the finding is troubling nonetheless.

The criminal justice data contain a number of troubling examples of disparities that don't seem to have obvious, race-neutral explanations. But it must be acknowledged that sometimes a disparity may *seem* to be attributable to something it's not *actually* a function of.

For example, consider a study on racial disparities in federal sentencing based on the political affiliations of judges.[15] The study found that Republican-appointed judges sentenced similarly situated Black defendants to three more months in prison than their Democrat-appointed counterparts. While this disparity might seem to support the inference that the result was driven by racial animus harbored by Republican-appointed judges, a deeper analysis seemed to undercut that theory. In *United States v. Booker*,[16] the Supreme Court ruled that the federal sentencing guidelines were advisory and no longer mandatory, giving federal judges significantly more discretion at the sentencing stage of criminal cases. The *Booker* decision fell within the observation period of this particular study, allowing for an assessment of its impact on disparities. Post-*Booker*, the racial disparities between sentences handed down by Republican- and Democrat-appointed judges during the study period doubled in magnitude.[17] "Importantly, however," noted the authors, "the increase in the racial gap by political affiliation is due to Democratic-appointed judges reducing their sentencing of black versus non-black offenders in the immediate aftermath of *Booker*, rather than Republican-appointed judges increasing their sentencing of black versus non-black offenders post-*Booker*."[18]

Were Republican-appointed judges itching to stick it to Black defendants, one would think they would have jumped at the opportunity to do so once the constraints of the sentencing guidelines were lifted. Indeed, the study concluded that the racial gaps in sentencing could not be fully explained by observable judge characteristics other than political affiliation, including "proxies for racial bias."[19]

## DRUG ENFORCEMENT AND RACIAL POLITICS

Controlling for relevant factors doesn't always entirely eliminate statistical disparities, but that doesn't always mean what remains can be attributed to racism. Methodological approaches matter too. Take, for instance, the last of the three examples bulleted at the top of this chapter: Analyses showing that Black people are arrested for drug offenses at higher rates than white people despite similar rates of use (and, in some cases, dealing), which are not devoid of controls. Use and distribution rates would, at first glance, seem to be highly relevant factors that the analysis clearly takes into account. But the analytical approach suffers from an important flaw in that it makes an assumption as to the social objectives being pursued through drug arrests. It assumes that arrests should be based on use or distribution rates. But what if that's not necessarily a given? What if it's just plain wrong?

Like other police enforcement activity—resource deployment, pedestrian stops, arrests, and so forth—drug arrests are often effected in service of an end not clearly tied to use or distribution rates. That end is violent crime reduction.

A good way to understand a significant portion of modern-day drug enforcement is as a pretextual attack on violent crime—something other analysts on both sides of the criminal justice debate have recognized.[20]

Over the course of a typical year, the overwhelming majority of serious felonies go "uncleared"—that is, they don't result in an arrest. For the violent index offenses tracked by the FBI (murder, robbery, rape, and aggravated assault), only 45.5 percent were cleared by law enforcement officers in 2018.[21] That number was just 17.6 percent for the property index offenses tracked by the bureau (larceny theft, motor vehicle theft, burglary, and arson).[22] Unlike these more serious offenses, drug offenses are engaged in at much higher rates. So, to the extent there is a significant degree of overlap between those that commit drug offenses and more serious violent crimes, police can theoretically make a dent in violence by focusing some of their resources on drug enforcement in high-crime segments of a given jurisdiction and on individuals suspected of more serious criminal activity.

Data points that suggest the overlap between drug and violent offenders is indeed quite significant include the following:

- In his 2017 book, *Locked In*, law professor John Pfaff highlighted a 1997 survey of state prison inmates in which more than 1 in 5 respondents serving time for a drug charge reported either "having used a firearm in a previous crime," or having had "prior convictions for violent crimes."[23]

- In 2017, Baltimore police identified 118 murder suspects, 70 percent of whom had at least one prior drug arrest.[24]

- A longitudinal study of recidivism among released state prisoners found that more than three-quarters of those incarcerated primarily for drug offenses went on to be rearrested for a *non-drug* crime—more than one-third were rearrested for a violent crime, specifically.[25]

One can certainly quarrel with the morality or advisability of pursuing violent crime reductions through drug enforcement, but the practice drastically undercuts the notion that disparities in drug enforcement data (even those that remain after controlling for use and distribution rates) are obviously a function of racism.

That assertion is doubly undercut by the role that minorities *themselves* played in the escalation of the drug war. Citing polling data from Gallup and Harris, criminologist Barry Latzer noted in his 2016 book, *The Rise and Fall of Violent Crime in America*, that by the end of the 1980s, "African Americans were *more* inclined toward punitiveness for drug use than whites by 38 to 32 percent"[26] (emphasis added). This, he noted, was not particularly surprising, given that Black neighborhoods "were paying the lion's share of the price" of the crime uptick driven by the crack epidemic. A look at the passage of the now infamous (for its establishment of the 100:1 sentencing disparity between crack and powder cocaine) Anti-Drug Abuse Act of 1986[27] illustrates the punitive answer to the crime question arrived at by so many in America's Black communities. The Anti-Drug Abuse Act—which sailed through both houses of Congress—was co-sponsored by 16 of the 19 members of the Congressional Black Caucus.[28] Other co-sponsors included then senator Joe Biden, former Ku Klux Klan member and then senator Robert Byrd, then senator Strom Thurmond, and then representative Charles Schumer.

Black support for the Anti-Drug Abuse Act shouldn't be surprising in light of the role Black middle-class communities played in passing similar laws in New York—known collectively as the Rockefeller Drug Laws—a decade earlier.[29]

Why did so many in America's Black communities participate in the escalation of a drug war that would produce such stark racial disparities? For the same reason police and prosecutors will concentrate drug enforcement efforts in violent neighborhoods and on those suspected of driving that violence. Drug-related violence ravaged America's Black communities to a degree not seen in other parts of the country. As Charles Murray noted in his seminal 1984 book, *Losing Ground: American Social Policy, 1950–1980*, "it was much more dangerous to be black in 1972 than it was in 1965, whereas it was not much more dangerous to be white."[30] The disparate impact of drug-related violent crime became even more pronounced once crack hit the streets in the mid-1980s. Indeed, the Black homicide victimization rate jumped 44 percent between 1984 and 1991.[31]

Acknowledging the history of Black communities vis-à-vis the issue of crime helps contextualize at least some of the disparities we see in the drug enforcement data, showing them to be partly a function of policy shifts that themselves were the result of concerns about violent crime. Those concerns were particularly pronounced within Black communities, whose activism helped bring about the changes in drug policy that exacerbated many of the disparities that would later be pointed to as evidence of racism.

## THE OTHER SIDE OF THE LEDGER

Through the early 1990s, violent crime had proven itself to be one of the most (if not *the* most) important domestic policy problems in America. By the end of the 1990s, the decline in violent crime constituted one of the most impressive and historic conquests of a governmental effort to address a widespread social problem. Patrick Sharkey—a sociologist whose work has focused on the role of crime in society—noted in his 2018 book, *Uneasy Peace: The Great Crime Decline, the Renewal of City Life, and the Next War on Violence*, that in 1993, according to the National Crime Victimization Survey, "about 80 out of every 1,000 Americans reported being the victim of a violent crime in the six months prior to the survey," but by 2015, that number was down to "only 19 out of every 1,000."[32] That drop-off represents a remarkable decline of more than 76 percent.

Given the geographic and demographic concentration of crime documented throughout this book, you should take a moment to internalize the fact that the sharp decline in violent crime (and the benefits that attended it) wasn't felt equally across America. The decline and its benefits were most pronounced in the pockets of concentrated violence where a disproportionate amount of the carnage of the 1970s, 1980s, and 1990s took place. While many of those places may still see a disproportionate amount of today's serious violent crime, many (though not all) of them are much better off today than they were then.

Salient to the topic of this chapter, however, is the disproportionate representation of Black and Latino people living in the pockets of concentrated violence that saw the steepest declines in shootings, homicides, robberies, and so forth.

In other words, just as America's Black and brown communities suffered the lion's share of the uptick in violence that peaked in the early 1990s, they also enjoyed an equally disproportionate share of the benefits that attended the sharp declines in violent crime that followed. The data out of New York City are quite illustrative on this point. In 1993, the gun-related homicide victimization rate for Black New Yorkers was just under 40 per 100,000; by 1999, it had dropped to about 10 per 100,000. By contrast, the white gun-related homicide victimization rate went from about 3 per 100,000 to about 1 per 100,000.

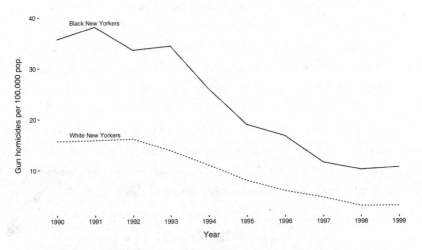

**Figure 5. Gun Homicide Rates in the Five Boroughs (1990–1999)**
*Source: Preeti Chauhan et al., "Race/Ethnic-Specific Homicide Rates in New York City: Evaluating the Impact of Broken Windows Policing and Crack Cocaine Markets," Homicide Studies, August 2011.*

Sharkey put it masterfully: "[T]he decline in American homicide has not had a dramatic effect on the health of the entire population, because violence is a phenomenon that is not common for most of the population. But for the most disadvantaged segment of the American population, black men, violence is the most urgent health crisis, and the crime decline is the most important public health breakthrough of the past several decades."[33]

To illustrate the significance of that breakthrough, Sharkey noted that "the impact of the decline in homicide on the life expectancy of black men is roughly equivalent to the impact of eliminating obesity altogether."[34] He went on, "For every 100,000 black men, over 1,000 more years of time with friends and family have been preserved because of the drop in the murder rate."

One of the reasons I admire some of Sharkey's work—despite sharply disagreeing with his policy prescriptions[35]—is that he has, perhaps better than anyone else in the field today, documented that the costs of violent crime (and, by extension, the benefits of violent crime declines) go well beyond questions of physical health and damage to the immediate victim. He and his colleagues have documented the toll that such crimes take on communities, affecting everything from upward economic mobility to school performance, which means that the data presented above capture only a slice of the benefits that inured to Black and brown communities because of the crime decline.

## WHAT ABOUT REFORMS?

Another reality that's incongruous with the idea that the criminal justice system is racist is the electoral and policy success of the reform movement—particularly with respect to changes rooted in concerns about systemic racism. As was highlighted earlier in the book, the "progressive" prosecutor movement gained considerable momentum in the wake of former St. Louis County prosecuting attorney Robert McCulloch's decision not to indict former Ferguson police officer Darren Wilson in the shooting death of Michael Brown. Today, more than 40 million Americans live in jurisdictions with "progressive" prosecutors who have used their offices to implement policies called for in the name of racial justice—lower rates of pretrial detention, more pretrial diversion, and less aggressive bargaining tactics.[36]

In recent years, significant levels of decarceration have been achieved through legislative reforms, cultural shifts within the broader judiciary, and shifts in priorities for police and prosecutors. Black people, in particular, have benefited greatly from these reforms—at least if you leave crime aside. According to the Pew Research Center, between 2006 and 2018, the Black incarceration rate declined by 34 percent, going from 2,261 per 100,000 to 1,501 per 100,000.[37] For Hispanic people, the decline was 25 percent over the same period.[38] The white incarceration rate, by contrast, declined just 17 percent over the 12-year period—the same as the percentage decline in the overall incarceration rate.[39]

The 100:1 sentencing disparity between crack and powder cocaine codified by the Anti-Drug Abuse Act of 1986 was undone by the Fair Sentencing Act of 2010, which reduced the disparity to 18:1 and eliminated mandatory minimums for crack possession, which closed much of the gap between the average sentences for offenses involving crack versus powder cocaine.[40] And New York's Rockefeller Drug Laws underwent significant reforms in the first decade of the 2000s, leading to reductions in racial disparities regarding post–drug arrest incarcerations.[41]

And in the wake of George Floyd's death in the custody of Minneapolis police, municipalities around the country acted swiftly (if misguidedly) to "defund" their police departments[42] and enact various reforms. In New York, Governor Andrew Cuomo signed a package of 10 police reform bills into law within weeks of Floyd's death,[43] and in late 2020, New Jersey's attorney general unilaterally implemented sweeping limits on police use of force.[44]

Surely, these changes have cut into the disproportionality seen in the data regarding at least some criminal justice outcomes. At the very least, as to the outcomes with disparities that remain unchanged, these reforms have still reduced the amount of harm inflicted by those outcomes, which now occur in smaller numbers. But even if neither of these things is true, the fact that these reform efforts have been successful should at least be reflected in the tone and substance of the debate about systemic racism in American criminal justice. The problem is that it doesn't seem to be.

## CONCLUSION

Those prosecuting the case against American criminal justice on the charge of systemic racism tend to focus almost exclusively on racial disparities in enforcement outcomes—arrests, incarceration rates, sentence lengths, and so forth—as if such data reflect the only outputs of the country's criminal justice systems. Doing so leaves their analysis incomplete insofar as they ignore the most important outputs of America's criminal justice system over the last 30 years: the massive crime declines experienced in so many

American cities. It's not just the fact of the crime declines that they fail to incorporate into their analysis; it's the fact that those declines were the explicitly stated *goals* of those at the helms of the various institutions of America's criminal justice system. In cities across the country, police chiefs, district attorneys, lawmakers, cops, prosecutors, and judges dedicated themselves to a mission of crime control. And the declines are consistently cited by defenders of these institutions as a treasured success.[45]

How is this relevant to the issue of systemic racism in American criminal justice? Because the people who benefited most from the nation's relatively recent crime declines are precisely the people we're told are singled out by the system for unfair treatment.

The unequal distribution of the benefits of crime-fighting complicates the argument of police critics regarding this issue because there isn't a good explanation for why a system allegedly rigged against and operated to the detriment of Black and brown Americans would *benefit* Black and brown Americans almost exclusively when the system attains the goals set by those at its helm.

Again, there is no doubt that justice has proved elusive in some cases for some people. Some of those injustices are the product of racial prejudices held by individual prosecutors, police officers, corrections officials, and judges. But if we are going to have a meaningful discussion about whether the impact America's criminal justice system has had on minority communities justify the charge of racism, we must weigh the disproportionality evident in the distribution of the *benefits* of the crime declines achieved through policing, prosecution, and incarceration against the disproportionality evident in the distribution of the costs of enforcement.

# CONCLUSION

**B**efore I deliver my closing argument, if you will, there are a couple of things I want to remind you, the reader, of.

First, while I have spent many years covering criminal justice issues and delving into the relevant empirical research, I remain a journalist formally trained in the law—not a criminologist, law enforcement practitioner, or econometrician. As such, it is possible I have overlooked or misinterpreted something that someone with a PhD in criminology or years of experience as an investigator wouldn't have. While you should feel free to hold any such mistakes (which I hope are few and far between) against me, I humbly ask that you nevertheless remain open to the possibility that they do not extirpate the broader arguments advanced. Even if this book ends up being completely free of any analytical errors, you can be certain that your investigation of these issues will be incomplete if it stops here. Many important books, essays, and studies—some mentioned herein, some not—have been (and will be) written on these topics by other scholars, journalists, and public intellectuals. Try to read more of them as you form your own opinions about how best to reform America's criminal justice system. Doing so can only help you better understand what has gone wrong and how best to proceed.

Second, I want to highlight an important caveat: Not all of the arguments addressed in this book are completely wrong; nor is every single one of the claims upon which I push back entirely false. As I have noted, there are a number of people who have been unnecessarily incarcerated and/or unjustifiably molested by police. However, that there is some truth to an observation does not automatically render true and noble the arguments and policy goals that flow from that observation. What I wanted to show in this book was that there are far too many holes in the cases for mass decarceration and depolicing to justify the approach to reform that has been taken over the last several years.

That approach has been characterized by, among other things (in no particular order):

- The election of "progressive" prosecutors and their adoption of broad non-prosecution and diversion policies.

- The administrative or legislative placement of broad restrictions on pretrial detention and release conditions.

- The proliferation of more lenient sentencing and parole practices.

- The erosion of police budgets.

- The demonization of the policing profession in the mainstream media.

- The expansion of federal interventions in local policing.

Put bluntly, recent criminal justice reform efforts have largely lowered the transaction costs of crime commission and raised the transaction costs of crime fighting. This can prove a dangerous combination of endeavors, which is why it's critical that we closely examine the ideas informing those dual pursuits.

Having gotten that out of the way, it's worth revisiting the goals of this book. When I sat down to write it, I set out to accomplish two things:

1. I wanted to illustrate and explore, through data and stories, the faulty assumptions, incomplete ideas, and factual errors undergirding many of the popular arguments made in service to a policy agenda built around the ideas that mass decarceration and depolicing are so central to the pursuit of justice—and such low-risk propositions—that they should be considered public policy goods unto themselves.

2. I wanted to establish that perhaps the biggest risk associated with mass decarceration and depolicing programs—an increase in serious crime—will be disproportionately borne by those already absorbing the lion's share of America's existing violent crime problem, which has gotten significantly worse in many of the country's already-troubled urban enclaves since 2015.

Let's start with the first of these.

As was noted in chapters 2 and 3, many critics of America's modern incarceration practices have sought to make out a prima facie case of a "mass incarceration" problem by leaning into the delta between America's incarceration rate and those of other nations—particularly other Western European democracies. Implicit in this critique is the goal of reducing incarceration until the US has achieved parity with other "developed" nations around the world. To do that, the United States would have to cut its incarceration rate by about 70 percent, which can only be done by releasing and refusing to incarcerate those who commit (and will continue to commit) serious violent offenses.[1] This is a dangerous policy goal, the pursuit of which has caused, and will likely continue to cause, real harm in the form of otherwise avoidable criminal victimizations. The reason for this is that—contrary to conventional wisdom that American prisons are teeming with petty thieves and nonviolent drug offenders—incarceration in the United States is already largely reserved for serious, violent, prolific offenders. Releasing or refusing to incarcerate so many American prisoners risks the safety of those in the communities in which those offenders spend their time. Another piece of conventional wisdom is that decarceration would benefit the children of those spared stints in jail and prison. But as is shown in chapter 4, a good bit of evidence seems to show that because so many prisoners are highly antisocial, their children may actually be better off without them around.

Decarceration is only one of two major planks of the modern criminal justice reform movement. The other is depolicing. For as long as I can remember, controversial use of force incidents—both excessive and lawful—have driven enormous amounts of public anger. Those incidents have been regularly seized upon (by anti-police activists and well-meaning reform advocates alike) to advance proposals to limit the duties and powers of police. After the murder of George Floyd in 2020, depolicing advocates enjoyed widespread success as local, state, and federal policymakers advanced new restrictions on American police. It's not at all clear, however, that those restrictions will make things better—that is, that the reforms advanced will significantly reduce the sorts of force incidents that led to their adoption. As chapter 5 makes clear, this is unlikely. Why? For one thing, the frequency of police uses of force is fantastically overstated. For another, the evidence that popular reform proposals are capable of significantly reducing already rare occurrences—at least without significantly risking the public's safety—is thin.

One key to the push for mass decarceration and depolicing is the idea that we can adequately address crime through non–law enforcement methods, because crime has its roots in economic deprivation. Chapter 1 outlines the lack of correlation between socioeconomic status markers and violent crime and highlights a stronger connection between violent criminality and other problems—like antisocial dispositions and substance use disorders—that you can't adequately alleviate by just giving people more money to spend. By contrast, there is a trove of evidence, outlined primarily in chapters 2, 3, and 5, showing that both policing and incarceration can more reliably prevent and reduce crime.

Another key to the push is the misconception that the statistical overrepresentation of Black and brown men in the data on stops and frisks, arrests, uses of force, and incarcerations constitutes clear evidence of racism that is both baked into the system and animates police, prosecutors, judges, and the like. However, there is a mountain of evidence highlighted throughout this book, but especially in chapter 7, that counters this point. That chapter argues that the racial disparities apparent in various enforcement measures must be viewed in their proper context. Part of that means asking whether there are race-neutral reasons for why those disparities exist. What we see when relevant factors are controlled for is that the disparities in enforcement are drastically reduced. Among those relevant factors is the geographic and demographic concentration of violent crime commission and victimization highlighted in chapter 1, which informs (among other things) how police resources are deployed. Those data also impact other measures (like sentencing outcomes) that vary with the extensiveness of an offender's criminal history.

The unequal distribution of crime doesn't just help explain the unequal distribution of police attention and enforcement; it also tells us that those living in the communities most affected by crime stand to benefit the most from the sorts of crime reductions we know from experience and research that data-driven policing and incarceration can provide. Those reductions come with real public health, economic, and social benefits that must be considered when confronted with arguments about the unequal distribution of law enforcement's costs.

While many of the arguments advanced in this book rely heavily on data, the reality is that even the most sophisticated econometricians will never be able to fully capture the impact of crime spikes or reductions because data can never fully capture the truly brutal nature of serious criminal violence or the impact it has on those affected. As I put it in a January 2021 piece for the *New York Times*, "Statistics are poor stand-ins for the lives cut short, the families torn apart, and the innocence stolen from the souls of children—like the 6-year-old girl whose father was gunned down right before her eyes as they crossed a Bronx street [in 2020], hand in hand, in broad daylight."[2] Three men were later charged in the slaying, and all three are said to have been indicted in a gang-related conspiracy case just a few years earlier.[3] Two of the three were, according to one news source, out on parole at the time of the shooting.[4]

The inability of statistics to fully capture the dark realities of criminal homicide was something I began to appreciate at the very young age of 11 when I decided to sneak a peek through my father's briefcase when he wasn't home. My father was a New York City Detective working in Brooklyn's 67th precinct at the time, and the idea of being a professional crimefighter was fascinating to me. But I always had the sense that he had only ever shared a fraction of the things he'd seen. My little dig through his briefcase confirmed it. I remember pulling out a manila file folder and noticing that behind some paperwork and handwritten notes that didn't look too interesting there was thin stack of photos. What they showed was the corpse of a Black man who seemed to have been shot multiple times at close range. He was slumped over on the floor with his back up against the wall. He was shirtless, and his chest and shoulder had been torn apart, revealing pink and white flesh that stood in stark contrast to his dark skin and the deep red pool of blood that had been drying on the floor. I'll never forget how swollen his face was. It was all I could do not to throw up on my parents' bedroom floor.

I spent the next few nights desperately trying to push the images out of my head, wishing I could ask my dad about what I knew I wasn't meant to see—all as more and more questions swirled around in my head. *Who could even stomach doing this to another human being? Was my dad supposed to catch the perpetrator(s)? And if so, was he in even more danger than I had thought? How often did cops have to see things like that? And how could anyone (cops or not) confront this level of barbarism on a regular basis and stay sane?*

As I write this, I think about how sickened I was at the age of 11 by the mere two-dimensional image of a dead body, and my heart absolutely aches for the six-year-old girl I mentioned in the *Times*. Not only was she made to *personally* witness the sort of callous evil I could only try to imagine, but the person whose body was torn up by bullets was her father's, who she was alone with at the time. Just try to imagine the shock, fear, grief, and psychological trauma that little girl endured as she stood in the middle of a busy street with no idea where to go as her father lay lifelessly in the crosswalk, bleeding out. How could she ever recover from that?

Focusing on data is important when engaging in criminal justice policy debates, but it can be all too easy to lose sight of the horrific realities of deadly violence. Keeping those realities in mind reminds us of what's at stake for those who the data make clear stand to lose the most if the risks of decarceration and depolicing come to pass.

# ACKNOWLEDGMENTS

Though I am writing this before having seen a single review, I can nevertheless say with confidence that the publication of *Criminal (In)Justice* represents an enormous accomplishment for me. But as with most major accomplishments, this book reflects a small part of what has been a long journey—one facilitated by the love, support, and guidance given to me by so many of my family members, friends, and colleagues. It would be impossible for me to acknowledge every single one of the people who has played a role in my personal, intellectual, and professional development. Nevertheless, I shall risk an important omission by naming just a few.

First and foremost, I'd like to thank my wife, Joyanet Mangual. Getting this book over the finish line meant many weekends and long nights spent in the office, adding so much to her already packed plate. Unfazed and indefatigable, Joy has picked up my slack without skipping a beat. She did all this while caring for our two-year-old son and expertly managing her own incredibly demanding career—all of which she did while pregnant with our daughter. Yet she still found the time to listen to me read every last word of this book to her out loud and give me feedback.

I'd also like to thank my parents, Rafael and Altagracia Mangual, and my sister, Matil Mangual Gutierrez, for all the help they gave to Joy and me throughout this process.

Beyond their more practical assistance, I'd also like to thank my parents for setting an incredible example for me to follow in life and for always working to instill in me an appreciation for education—even when I was determined to resist their efforts. Given the topic of this book, it's only right that I specially recognize my dad, who, thanks to his more than 20 years of service in the NYPD, gave me important insights that I've benefited from in my coverage of these issues over the years—years spent at the Manhattan Institute, my professional home throughout my still-developing career in public policy.

Spending my days thinking about the issues I care deeply about and exchanging ideas with the brilliant public intellectuals I get to call colleagues has been such a gift. For that, I'd like to thank the Institute's president, Reihan Salam, executive vice president Ilana Golant, and vice president for public policy, Brandon Fuller, who have been so incredibly supportive of my work. I'd be remiss not to also thank former Manhattan Institute president Larry Mone, former executive vice president Vanessa Mendoza, and former vice president for public policy Troy Senik for their help and support throughout my first few years at the Manhattan Institute.

I first came to the Institute as a member of its legal policy team, working under my colleague, friend, and mentor James "Jim" Copland. In addition to being one of the smartest people I've ever met, Jim is also one of the most gracious. From the moment I arrived, Jim took a sincere interest in helping me achieve my goals and never hesitated to extend an opportunity to take something on—even when I wasn't sure I could.

In addition to my work as a senior fellow and head of research, I am also privileged to be on *City Journal*'s prestigious roster of contributing editors. Since I was about 19, I have regarded *City Journal* as the country's best magazine. It wasn't until I began writing for it that I learned why it is so consistently good. Editor Brian Anderson and managing editor Paul Beston have, through their patient and meticulous editing of my work over the years, taught me a great deal about how to write—lessons that would be apparent to anyone given the chance to compare some of my early submissions to my most recent ones.

I also want to take a moment to thank a late colleague that I knew all too briefly. George L. Kelling was a giant in his field. His contributions to the literature on policing were so incredibly influential to my own thinking—something I know is true for countless others. Giving me some of my most cherished professional memories, George and his wonderful wife and collaborator, Catherine Coles, opened their home to me on multiple occasions in the twilight of George's life. The many hours I spent in their living room and on the phone with them assisting George with what would be his final piece of published work had such an enormous impact on me. In addition to talking me through some of his ideas, George gave me so much encouragement to pursue my own writing, which meant the world coming from him. George also introduced me to Commissioner William "Bill" Bratton, from whom I have also learned so much.

All of the colleagues I just mentioned (along with others I left out) have been so instrumental in getting me to the point of feeling like I could write a book. And when a Manhattan Institute fellow gets to that point, there is someone there to help guide them through the process. That someone is the Institute's book director, Bernadette Serton, whom I'd like to thank for her help and support with everything from putting together the proposal to thinking through how to write each chapter. Especially when it comes to books about public policy debates, the writing process is preceded by an enormous amount of research. And while any and all errors should be attributed solely to me, I do want to thank a few other people for their research assistance, collegial support, and their great work, which has informed my own: Hannah Meyers, Charles Fain Lehman, Robert VerBruggen, Mia Chiba, and Noah Muscente (as well as his wife, Kailee Kodama Muscente).

Because the Manhattan Institute and those who call it home have been so central to my work, I must also take a moment to thank those who make our work possible through their philanthropic support. In particular, I'd like to thank the Paul E. Singer Foundation, the Arthur N. Rupe Foundation, and Mr. Nick Ohnell for their generous support of the Institute's Policing and Public Safety Initiative and of this project, specifically.

Of course, when you're trying to get a book published, it helps to have some visibility in the media, for which I must thank the Manhattan Institute's communications team: Michele Jacob, Nora Kenney, and Leah Thomas. It also helps to have a hired gun, and so I'd like to thank mine: literary agent extraordinaire Andrew Stuart, to whom I'm so grateful for believing in me as a first-time author and for helping a number of competing publishers see what he saw—which takes me to the team at Center Street. First, I want to thank Daisy Hutton and Sean

McGowan (who has since moved on professionally) for acquiring this book. I'd also like to thank Center Street editorial director Alex Pappas and my editor, Kathryn Riggs, for shepherding this project through the publication process, taking it from an idea to a finished product.

Again, this is just a short version of what is a much longer list of people who have played roles—direct and indirect, small and large—in my development. I will be forever grateful to you all.

## Testimony before the US Senate Committee on the Judiciary's Subcommittee on Criminal Justice and Counterterrorism

*April 22, 2021*

I'D LIKE TO THANK the subcommittee for the invitation to deliver testimony. It is an honor and a privilege to address this body on an issue that is among the most important public policy debates of our time. Unfortunately, it's also among the most divisive.

Much of the conversation about how to reform policing in the United States seems to be driven by a key misperception: that police violence is a likely outcome of an investigative or enforcement interaction—particularly when those interactions involve people of color. For example, in a report released by the Manhattan Institute earlier this month, political scientist Eric Kaufmann found that eight in ten African American survey respondents "believe that young Black men are more likely to be shot to death by the police than to die in a traffic accident," and "among a highly educated sample of liberal Whites, more than 6 in 10 agreed."[1] A 2016 Morning Consult poll found that twice as many Black respondents reported worrying about those they know becoming victims of police brutality than of gun violence, generally.[2]

But these beliefs are completely at odds with the data on police use of force. A recent study published in the *Proceedings of the National Academy of Sciences* shows that young Black men (between the ages of twenty-five and twenty-nine) are killed by police "at a rate between 2.8 and 4.1 per 100,000," which is far lower than the rate at which they die in traffic accidents.[3] That same study put the odds of dying at the hands of police at 1 in 1,000 for Black men. Contrast that with the odds for all Americans (i.e., of any race) of being killed by gun assault, which, according to the National Safety Council, are dramatically higher at 1 in 298.[4] Given that Black men are more than ten times more likely than their white counterparts to be the victim of a homicide, it's quite clear that their risk of death at the hands of police is far lower than their risk of being killed by gun violence, generally.

And while 83 percent of respondents to a Pew Research survey guessed that the typical police officer has fired his gun at least once on the job, only about 1 in 4 (27 percent) actually do.[5]

In reality, police very rarely use force; and when they do, it very rarely results in serious injury.

In 2018, police officers in the US discharged their firearms an estimated 3,043 times.[6] That year, they made more than 10.3 million criminal arrests.[7] Attributing each of the 3,043 estimated firearm discharges by police in 2018 to a unique officer would mean that, at most, 0.4 percent of officers purposely discharged a firearm in 2018, and assuming that every shooting happened during the course of a separate arrest would mean that, at most, police applied deadly force with a firearm in just 0.003 percent of arrests.[8]

As to nondeadly force, in 2018, a research team of doctors and a criminologist published a thorough study of police use of force in the *Journal of Trauma and Acute Care Surgery.*[9] The study analyzed more than a million calls for service to three midsized police departments in Arizona, Louisiana, and North Carolina over a two-year period. Those calls resulted in more than 114,000 arrests. Physical force was used in 1 of every 128 of them, meaning that more than 99 percent of arrests were effected without any use of force.[10] The study went on to find, based on expert medical examinations of suspects' medical records, that 98 percent of suspects on whom police used physical force "sustained no or mild injury," and 1.8 percent of suspects sustained moderate or severe injuries (only one suspect was fatally wounded by police gunfire during the study period).[11]

Nor are uses of force likely when you drill down into particularly dangerous police encounters or encounters involving those in crisis. Take my home city of New York for example. In 2020, the NYPD made 20,935 arrests of suspects who possessed weapons.[12] They also responded to 161,278 911 calls for persons in crisis.[13] Yet the department recorded just 42 firearm discharges in 2020, including off-duty shootings.[14] It would seem that, by and large, police are generally pretty skilled at dealing with dangerous and/or unstable subjects without relying on brute force.

Of course, none of this means that there isn't room for improvement, or that police are perfect. There is, and they're not. Exploring opportunities for reform is a worthwhile endeavor, but it's one that must be undertaken soberly, because pulling the wrong policy lever can have disastrous effects, particularly on crime. That's a risk we should be especially cognizant of now, given the sharp uptick in shootings and homicides across the country.

Last year, for the first time since 1995, criminologists have estimated, based on preliminary figures, that the US saw at least 20,000 criminal homicides—an increase of about 4,000 additional homicides compared to 2019.[15] While that's still a ways off from the nearly 25,000 homicides the country experienced in 1991,[16] some cities have seen their homicide numbers approach and even surpass their 1990s peaks. In 2020, Cleveland, Ohio, had its highest murder tally since 1982;[17] Minneapolis, Minnesota, had more murders than every year since 1995;[18] Cincinnati, Ohio, and Louisville, Kentucky, both set new homicide records.[19]

That uptick, it should be noted, was not evenly distributed. It was heavily concentrated in minority neighborhoods already struggling with elevated levels of crime. While many conversations about policing in America tend to focus heavily on racial disparities in various enforcement statistics, we should also remember that while people of color may bear a disproportionate share of the costs attributable to policing, the burden of serious violent crime increases is one that also falls disproportionately on the shoulders of people of color. In New York City, going back to at least 2008, a minimum of 95 percent of all shooting victims were either Black or Hispanic; 2020, which saw shootings spike 97 percent, was no exception.[20]

It has been well documented that policing can produce real societal benefits in the way of reduced crime. There are a number of strong studies done throughout the country over the course of many years that find additional policing to have significant crime-reduction effects. In laymen's terms, what those studies bear out is that, generally speaking, more police means less

crime.[21] And just as people of color—particularly Black men—
are disproportionately impacted by crime increases, they disproportionately benefit from crime declines. Between 1991 and
2014, the US experienced a sharp decline in homicides. A 2019
analysis of that decline showed that, during that period, "the
decline of homicide-specific mortality led to increases in [life
expectancy] of . . . 0.14 years for white males," versus "1.00 years
for African American males."[22] To contextualize that data point,
that same study's lead author wrote in his 2018 book that "the
impact of the decline in homicide on the life expectancy of black
men is roughly equivalent to the impact of eliminating obesity
altogether."[23]

Crime declines are often cited as examples of policing's
success by police executives, rank-and-file officers, and other
defenders of the institution. One question that might be worth
considering, given the rhetorical posture of the current debate
about American policing, is whether an institution whose stated
purpose (as stated by both those at its helm and its lower ranks) is
to produce outcomes that the evidence tells us disproportionately
benefits minorities can be fairly categorized as systemically racist
toward those very minority groups. The answer to the question
isn't simple. Black and Hispanic communities do bear disproportionately the costs of policing, including false-positive police
interventions, a phenomenon partly but probably not wholly
attributable to underlying variations in violent crime levels. But
at a minimum, if we're assessing the racial impact of policing, it's
important to look at both sides of the ledger—that is, not only at
the costs but also the benefits.

I suspect that sincerely held misperceptions about police have
shaped the overarching goal of the reform movement, which, at

the moment, seems to be to minimize the footprint of police (and the criminal justice system more broadly) in any way possible. We have heard calls to "defund" the police—which, in some cities, have been heeded. We have also heard calls to divert more responsibilities—particularly things like traffic enforcement and responding to mental health calls—away from police to unarmed civilians. The assumption is that this will reduce the scope of interactions that might result in tragedy. But even if that's true in the case of traffic enforcement, for example, it will also reduce the scope of interactions that might lead to the discovery of more serious criminal activity. In 1995, the National Institute of Justice published a study titled "The Kansas City Gun Experiment," which analyzed enforcement and deployment decisions targeted in hot spots for gun violence. Among the key findings, it was noted that, in the targeted beats, "Traffic stops were the most productive method of finding guns, with an average of 1 gun found in every 28 traffic stops."[24] What needs to be carefully considered is the reality that many "lower-level" interactions can and often do lead to the discovery of contraband, the closure of open warrants, and the recovery of illegal firearms. Zeroing out those encounters, therefore, will not be cost-free.

On the mental health front, there is some evidence to suggest that we should continue to invest in efforts to augment the police by deploying civilian crisis intervention teams to calls involving people in crisis. In a report released just yesterday, my Manhattan Institute colleague Charles F. Lehman reviews some of that evidence.[25] Among the approaches evaluated in that report is a popular, oft-cited, and promising effort launched in Eugene, Oregon, called CAHOOTS (Crisis Assistance Helping Out on the Streets). While effective, CAHOOTS is also a case study in the limits of programs loosely referred to as alternatives to policing. As Lehman notes in his report:

> CAHOOTS responders are highly specialized. In 2019, they covered just 17% of Eugene 911 calls, with 75% of those calls being a welfare check, providing transportation to someone (usually homeless or in need), or assisting the police already on the beat. Even in those relatively limited circumstances, CAHOOTS responders still called for backup in roughly one in every 67 calls for service in 2019.

It is hard to see that model scaling up to cover the other 83 percent of 911 calls to the Eugene PD. Doing so would involve not only dramatically scaling up CAHOOTS's $2.1 million budget but also identifying a large population of trained CIT professionals and, most significantly, asking those professionals to handle situations that grow increasingly risky as responsibility expands. In other words, though it doubtless provides a useful service now, groups like CAHOOTS are not a model for how to replace the police. But as a complement to policing, it may be a useful model for other cities to adopt.[26]

When you consider the sheer volume of mental health calls received by police (not to mention the fact that they're often received in the late-night or early-morning hours), it becomes clear that we simply don't have the capacity to shift this particular responsibility in total. Another complicating factor is that it is often unclear as to whether a call can be accurately categorized as one that can be safely diverted to civilian responders trained in mental health crises as opposed to police based on either 911 calls or dispatcher information. One study of such calls for service in the city of Philadelphia recently found "that some medical or public health activity initially masquerades as crime or other policing work and some events eventually determined to be police/crime activity can initially appear to be public health related."[27] The study went on to note that "[a]bout 20% of activity in this area does not appear predictable from the initial call type as handled by police dispatch."[28]

None of this is to say that improving outcomes in policing isn't something we should pursue with vigor. It is. I have outlined a number of reforms that would be worth pursuing in the short and long run,[29] and I will talk about some of those in my oral testimony. But while reform is a worthy pursuit, it cannot be allowed to cause us to lose sight of the government's first duty, which is to provide for the public's safety. As serious violent crime across American cities continues to rise in the first months of this year, that mission should be viewed as more critical than ever.

Thank you.

## Statement to the President's Commission on Law Enforcement: Working Group on Respect for Law Enforcement

*July 21, 2020*

### Misleading Narratives about Incarceration, Prosecution, and Policing: Drivers of the Decline in Respect for Law Enforcement and the Rule of Law

COMMISSIONERS, ATTORNEY GENERAL BARR, and distinguished members of the commission, I would like to thank you all for the invitation to deliver remarks here today on what is a deeply important topic. My name is Rafael A. Mangual, and I am a fellow and deputy director of legal policy at the Manhattan Institute for Policy Research, where I have worked since 2015, focusing mostly on issues relating to criminal justice.[1] While my remarks will draw heavily on the work I have done while at the Manhattan Institute, my statement here today is solely my own, and not that of my employer.

Today's topic—the diminishing respect for law enforcement and the rule of law—is one that is dear to my heart. It's also one I have closely observed as a writer. The title of the hearing actually describes a trend. That trend seems to me to be the product of false or misleading narratives about incarceration and policing in the United States. That those narratives are false or misleading is itself a serious problem. But that problem has been compounded by the fact that those narratives are informing meaningful political action (illustrated in part by the growth of the so-called progressive prosecutor movement), which has resulted in consequential changes in public policy—both through and outside the political process. The stakes involved in pulling these policy levers are high. In some cases, those stakes can be life and death.

I'd like to begin by illustrating those stakes with two brief vignettes, which I'll follow with an overview of what the prevailing narratives about American criminal justice get wrong, and how that has contributed to the diminishment in respect we're here to discuss.

The first is that of a young woman named Brittany Hill, who was gunned down on Chicago's West Side last year while shielding her one-year-old daughter. Hill's murder was captured on a security camera operated by the Chicago Police Department. That video showed her standing on the street one morning alongside two other men when a sedan slowly approached the group. Just after Hill's daughter waved to the sedan's occupants, the man in the passenger seat opened fire, wounding Hill just inches below where she was holding her daughter. Hill turned to shield the little girl, collapsing just a few feet away, still holding on to her daughter when she died.

Because of the video, police quickly apprehended the suspected shooters, both of whom, as was reported by the *Chicago Sun-Times*,[2] had extensive criminal histories and active criminal justice statuses at the time. One of the alleged shooters, Michael Washington, who was on parole, reportedly had "nine felony convictions, including for a 2004 second-degree murder charge and a 2001 battery charge that was reduced from attempted murder in a plea agreement." The other, Eric Adams, who was on probation for a gun charge, has a history of multiple arrests.

The second story I wanted to share is that of Robert Williams, who, in February of this year, is alleged to have shot and wounded two NYPD police officers in ambush attacks within the confines of the department's 41st Precinct. He was taken into custody at the scene of the second shooting, which was in the precinct's reception area. Williams is apparently no stranger to the justice system. The *New York Times* reported that Williams has multiple arrests dating to the mid-1990s, including a robbery charge when he was just fourteen.[3] After his sentencing in 1995, he was paroled twice. He subsequently returned to prison for violating his parole—twice. The *Times* also reported that Williams shot someone in 2002 and then carjacked a woman while fleeing. The shooting resulted in a conviction for attempted murder. Despite that conviction and the suspect's criminal history, Williams was released early from prison in 2017. Despite the leniency many would argue he had been shown, the *Times* reported that "Williams had told investigators in videotaped interviews that he carried out the attacks because 'he was tired of police officers.'"

In both of these cases, we have extremely violent repeat offenders on the street despite troubling criminal histories and convictions for serious gun-related offenses.

Not only do these stories illustrate the stakes involved in criminal justice policymaking, but they also undermine many of the claims we so often hear in debates about criminal justice reform—particularly the claim that the US is a draconian police state that regularly incarcerates relatively harmless offenders for years on end.

So let's get into some of those claims, beginning with incarceration. Here, I'd like to make two main points:

1. The international comparisons of incarceration cited as prima facie evidence that the US overincarcerates ignore essential differences that take the wind out of the comparison's rhetorical sails.
2. Contrary to conventional wisdom, incarceration is a relatively rare sanction, reserved mostly for violent and chronic offenders.

Let's start with number one. One of the most repeated lines at the front end of any argument about "mass incarceration" is that the United States is home to just 5 percent of the world's population, but houses a whopping 25 percent of the world's prisoners. What those who make this point don't tell you is that this disparity is almost entirely a function of differences that, when controlled for, significantly cushion the rhetorical blow that the comparison is usually intended to have.

The most obvious of those differences are found in the number and rate of serious crimes most likely to lead to lengthy prison sentences that are committed in the US. Take homicide, for instance, and consider the scope of that problem in England and Wales—one of the Western European democracies with a significantly lower incarceration rate with which the US is often unfavorably compared. As I recently wrote in an essay for the publication *Law and Liberty*,[4] England and Wales have a combined population of about 59 million people[5] and currently see 726 homicides a year (based on the year ending in March 2018).[6] Compare that with four contiguous community areas

(Humboldt Park, Austin, East Garfield Park, and West Garfield Park) on Chicago's West Side, which, in 2018, saw 121 homicides (16 percent of the total for England and Wales) despite housing an estimated population of just 189,846 (0.3 percent of the population of England and Wales).[7] The murder rate of those four community areas (63.73 per 100,000) is more than fifty times higher than that of England and Wales (1.23 per 100,000). Adding to the mix Baltimore's Western and Southwestern police districts, which, with a combined estimated population of 103,052, and 100 homicides in 2018,[8] would mean that just a few subsections of just *two* American cities see 30 percent of the homicides seen in the whole of England and Wales, despite those subsections having a combined population that (at 292,898) is just 0.5 percent of England and Wales.

Number two: In addition to out-of-context international comparisons, the "mass incarceration" meme posits that the US can be aptly described as a draconian carceral state that imprisons far too many people for far too many offenses, for far too long. Here again, the data don't support this conclusion. The first thing that often gets left out is that a prison sentence isn't exactly a given consequence of a felony conviction. Historically, only about 40 percent of state felony convictions result in a post-conviction prison sentence,[9] and the median prison sentence actually served is just about sixteen months.[10] Second, the majority (60 percent) of prisoners in the US are serving time primarily for one of just five serious offenses: murder (14.2 percent), rape or sexual assault (12.8 percent), robbery (13.1 percent), aggravated or simple assault (10.5 percent), and burglary (9.4 percent).[11]

Third is that contrary to what many believe—thanks to popular but misleading works like Michelle Alexander's *The New*

*Jim Crow*[12] and Ava DuVernay's Netflix film *13th*[13]—nonviolent drug offenders are most certainly *not* driving American incarceration. Those serving time primarily for drug offenses constitute less than 15 percent of state prisoners (who account for about 90 percent of the national prison population). Moreover, those who are primarily incarcerated for drug offenses tend not to spend much time in prison. Just under half (45 percent) of them are out within a year; and nearly 20 percent are out within six months.[14]

There is a reason I refer to those serving time *primarily* for drug offenses. Often obfuscated in these debates is that incarceration statistics usually categorize offenders based on the most serious charge of which they were convicted, which usually translates to the one for which they received the most time. Particularly given the fact that convictions are usually the products of plea bargains that result in dropped or reduced charges, one must understand that prison population categories don't tell the whole story. Three data points illustrate why this is particularly true for drug offenders: (1) According to the Bureau of Justice Statistics, more than three-quarters of released drug offenders are eventually rearrested for a *nondrug* crime;[15] (2) more than a third are rearrested for a violent crime, specifically; and (3) in Baltimore, seven in ten homicide suspects in 2017 had at least one prior drug arrest in their criminal histories.

So, why are all these clarifications important? One reason is that many of our most prominent lawmakers and political figures—including the presumptive Democratic Party nominee for president, have bought into the mass incarceration meme. Joe Biden has explicitly committed to pursuing a 50 percent reduction in incarceration as a result.[16] Another reason is that allowing the claims I've addressed here to stand gives American citizens a warped sense of what criminal justice actually looks like in the United States. One example of that can be found in an oft-touted ACLU poll showing that 71 percent of Americans believe we should reduce the prison population.[17] But when you contrast that poll's results with a 2016 Morning Consult poll, we begin to see the support for prison population reductions documented by the ACLU may be based on a misconception. It turns out that support for decarceration is significantly eroded when you ask specifically about those convicted of violent offenses and those who pose an elevated risk of reoffending. In fact, large majorities oppose measures to incarcerate *those* offenders less. As *Vox*'s German Lopez put it at the time, the poll showed that "voters overestimate how many people are in prison for nonviolent drug offenses while underestimating—or at least not knowing—that most of the growth in state prisons was driven by sentences for violent crime."[18]

But the misdirections and obfuscations I've examined so far do more than just lead voters to support misguided decarceration; they undermine respect for the very system we've designed to address serious lawbreaking by convincing the public that the system, by and large, produces results they find offensive.

When it comes to policing, we find much of the same. Now, it's important to recognize the context of our current moment. We are in the wake of a wave of violent protests following the extremely disturbing death of George Floyd under the knee of a former Minneapolis police officer. Everyone should be disturbed by the force exerted by Derek Chauvin against George Floyd, and there is no question that police *do* sometimes engage in unjustifiable abuses. However, the fact remains that one of the most pernicious claims advanced about police is illustrated by the oft-repeated claim that Black and Latino parents have to warn their children about police violence at a young age and coach them through how to minimize their chances of being brutalized. A version of that claim was repeated on ABC's *This Week* in 2014 by New York City mayor Bill de Blasio. So, little wonder that de Blasio's son, Dante, made the same assertion in a column for *USA Today* last year, lamenting the need for "young black people" to be taught (as he was) "to fear the people meant to protect us."[19] This idea is born out of the mistaken belief (fueled again by misrepresentations of the data) that police regularly use excessive force in their dealings with the public.

But on the whole, police use of force is extremely rare. Rarer still are uses of force that are injurious and unwarranted. In 2018, police in the United States discharged their firearms an estimated 3,043 times.[20] This may sound like a lot, but that number must be contextualized in light of the overall volume of police activity in the US. In 2018, more than 686,000 full-time law enforcement officers were working across America.[21] That year, officers made more than 10.3 million arrests[22] and had contact with more than 53 million people.[23] If we attribute each of the 3,043 estimated firearm discharges by police in 2018 to a unique officer, we can infer that, at most, 0.4 percent of police officers purposely discharged a firearm in 2018. If we assume that every shooting happened during the course of a separate arrest, we can infer that, at most, police applied deadly force with a firearm in 0.003 percent of arrests.

On the question of nondeadly use of force, a recent study published in the *Journal of Trauma and Acute Care Surgery* revealed that more than 99 percent of arrests by police are made without the use of physical force.[24] That study, undertaken by a team of doctors and criminologists, analyzed more than one million service calls to three midsized police departments in North Carolina, Louisiana, and Arizona. Those calls resulted in 114,064 criminal arrests. In making those arrests, police used force just 0.78 percent of the time, and when they did, they seemed to have exercised restraint, given that "among 914 suspects, 898 (98 percent) sustained no or mild injury after police UOF."

Ignoring these facts has allowed the misperception about police to persist, which has had real consequences—particularly for the populations the most vociferous police critics purport to represent. One illustration of those consequences comes from a study published in the *American Sociological Review*, which found that Black residents in particular were significantly less likely to call 911 after a controversial police use of force went viral.[25] The authors of that study attributed at least part of that reduction to an increase in "legal cynicism"—defined as "the deep-seated belief in the incompetence, illegitimacy, and unresponsiveness of the criminal justice system"—which, in turn, threatens the public's safety. More evidence of that cynicism may be found in another Morning Consult poll in which twice as many Black respondents reported worrying more about those they know becoming victims of police brutality than of gun violence[26]—a result at odds with a recent study published in the *Proceedings of the National Academy of Sciences*, which put the odds of dying at the hands of police at 1 in 1,000 for Black men.[27] Contrast that with the odds for *all Americans* of being killed by gun assault, which, according to the National Safety Council, are *dramatically* higher at 1 in 298.[28] With Black men more than ten times more likely than their white counterparts to be the victim of a homicide,[29] the risk of death at the hands of police is far lower than homicide generally.

It does not require a giant leap to conclude that such cynicism has eroded the public's respect for the policing profession and the system of laws they're sworn to uphold.

## CONCLUSION

The perpetuation of false narratives about policing and incarceration have emboldened some of the most radical elements of the criminal justice reform movements, such that once fringe ideas like the abolition of police and prisons are dramatically closer to the mainstream than they were just a year ago. Since the death of George Floyd, we've seen police departments around the country defanged in various ways, which has also emboldened the criminal class, whose members have taken advantage of the vacuum created by these "reforms." In my home city, we've seen a troubling uptick in shootings that portends a potential erosion of its nationally renowned success on the crime-fighting front. Through July 12, 2020, murders in New York City are up 23 percent year to date; shootings are up 61 percent.[30] The twenty-eight-day period ending July 12 saw 210 percent *more* shootings than the same period in 2019.[31] This is not just a short-term blip driven by the recent economic downturn. The two-year trend in shootings and homicides shows those crimes up 70 percent and 22 percent, respectively.[32] That crime increase, like crime more generally, is not evenly distributed. In East Harlem's 23rd Precinct, murders are up 500 percent year to date through July 12; shootings have doubled. In Harlem's 25th Precinct, murders are up 250 percent and shootings are up 400 percent. In the 73rd Precinct, which covers Brownsville, Brooklyn, murders have more than doubled year to date; shootings have increased by 215 percent. But in the Upper East Side's 19th Precinct, there has only been one shooting all year. The same goes for the 78th Precinct, which covers Mayor Bill de Blasio's neighborhood of Park Slope. This should serve as a reminder that, to the extent that radical reforms make life more dangerous, those dangers will disproportionately fall on America's most vulnerable communities.

When I prepared the first draft of my remarks for today, our country was dealing with the beginning of the novel coronavirus pandemic that, by April 1, 2020, had claimed more than 4,400 American lives—with New York State accounting for 44 percent of those deaths (and 41 percent of all cases in the US) at the time.[33] Despite New York being the epicenter of the COVID-19 pandemic in America in early April, police throughout the state continued their service, which, by definition, involved close contact with potentially infected members of the public—often with minimal protective gear. By April 1, more than one thousand NYPD officers had contracted the virus, with five losing their lives to it.[34] What the continued commitment of those officers showed is a deep commitment to the rule of law, which we know—from this pandemic, 9/11-related illness, and line-of-duty deaths and injuries—often comes at great personal cost to law enforcement officers. It's that commitment which should be painting the public image of the men and women who protect and serve communities across our great nation. That nearly a million officers across our nation have taken oaths to risk their lives in service to the rule of law should place that ideal among those most revered in our society.

People of good will can certainly disagree about the extent to which our criminal justice system—which is by no means perfect—is flawed, and they can disagree about how to go about improving that system. But the idea that our criminal justice system is fairly characterized as one that regularly brutalizes disfavored groups via overly draconian sentences and unjustifiably violent policing is nothing short of defamatory. So, to my mind, the best way to restore the respect that this group acknowledges has been lost is to fight innuendo with empiricism, obfuscation with analysis, lies with truth.

Thank you.

# Testimony before the US Commission on Civil Rights

*February 26, 2021*

I'D LIKE TO START by thanking the commissioners for the invitation to speak and submit written testimony. The issue of bail reform, like most issues of criminal justice, is an important one with major implications for both individual liberty and public safety. Drawing in part on my coverage of the bail reform debate in New York, this statement will make four points:

1. Pretrial justice systems that rely heavily on monetary conditions on release—i.e., cash bail—can, and sometimes do, place undue burdens on individual liberty, highlighting the need for reform.
2. Reform in this space should be approached with an eye toward mitigating the risks associated with eroding the incapacitation benefits that can be attributed to pretrial detention—particularly with respect to high-risk, high-rate offenders.
3. Because much of the concern surrounding the issue of bail reform is rooted in the amount of time presumably innocent defendants stand to spend in pretrial detention

(which, in turn, is almost entirely a question of resources), the federal government should consider providing financial assistance aimed at facilitating the quicker, more efficient processing of criminal cases at the state and local level—including the hiring of more judges, prosecutors, and public defenders, as well as the funding of research efforts aimed at developing and refining algorithmic risk assessment tools.

4. Typically, when an individual is arrested and charged with a crime, they are brought before a judge who will, among other things, decide whether and, if so, under what conditions the defendant will be released while their case runs its course. In jurisdictions that allow for the imposition of cash bail, the judge can, at least in some cases, require said defendant to post "a security such as cash or a bond . . . required by a court for the release of a prisoner who must appear in court at a future time." Depending on the jurisdiction, that requirement can be based on the judge's assessment of the risk that the defendant will fail to appear for their next court date, or that they will reoffend during the pretrial period.

When a judge imposes bail, the defendant can either pay the court in cash—which is then held in escrow and returned upon the defendant's return to court—or secure a bail bond by paying a bondsman a percentage of the bail amount. Basic economics teaches us that raising the price of anything will, at least in theory, price some people out of the particular market in question. Bail is no different. As such, in jurisdictions in which judges can impose financial conditions on a given defendant's release, there will inevitably be cases in which some defendants will be financially unable to post bail or secure a bail bond. Unless the bail amount is lowered to the point of affordability or someone else fronts the money, defendants who are financially unable to satisfy monetary conditions on their release will remain in pretrial detention. This is where the concerns animating so many proponents of bail reform begin to arise.

One of the most persuasive arguments against pretrial justice systems that rely heavily on cash bail is that such systems would allow for a dangerous but well-off defendant to secure his release, while a poor but harmless defendant remains in pretrial detention for an extended period of time. In other words, the problem with relying heavily on cash bail is that it makes the question of pretrial release one of means rather than one of risk. Such outcomes are unjust, and avoiding them is a proper aim of a bail reform effort.

However, as with almost any public policy decision, bail reform involves trade-offs. On one side of the scale, you have the defendant's liberty interests. On the other, you have the public's safety. Expanding pretrial release for its own sake inherently raises the risks to the public's safety, just as restricting pretrial release for its own sake raises the risks to the liberty interests of criminal defendants. Because so much concern and attention has been directed toward mitigating the latter risk, I'd like to focus a bit on the former.

One thing the research on bail reform seems to pretty convincingly show is that an increase in the percentage of pretrial defendants released pending trial will translate to more crimes committed by that population. One study by researchers at Princeton, Harvard, and Stanford Universities found that pretrial release increases the likelihood of rearrest prior to case disposition by more than 37 percent—it also increased the likelihood of a defendant failing to appear in court by 124 percent, which adds to the burden of police officers tasked with returning absconders to court. Two other studies analyzing the recent bail reform effort in Chicago also found increases in the number of crimes committed by pretrial defendants in that jurisdiction. In a study of violent felons convicted in large urban counties between 1990 and 2002, the Bureau of Justice Statistics found that 12 percent of those felons were out on pretrial release at the time of their arrests.

To put a finer point on the public safety stakes of this debate, consider the story of sixteen-year-old Kahlik Grier, who was shot and killed last month in the Bronx, New York, while in the stairwell of his own apartment building. One of the people charged with his murder is a nineteen-year-old suspect named Desire Louree, who, according to news reports, had been released from jail after making bail a month prior to the shooting. At the time of Grier's death, reports state that Louree had open cases for gun possession and attempted murder—the former from 2019, and the latter stemming from a shooting in Brooklyn last year. Consider also the case of Arjun Tyler, another New York City defendant who allegedly attempted to rape a woman in Brooklyn not long after being released from pretrial detention pursuant to New York's relatively recent bail reform.

These victims also have liberty interests that should be given due consideration in debates about bail reform. Minimizing the risks faced by those with the highest likelihood of being victimized by pretrial defendants who reoffend is as worthy a cause as protecting the liberty interests of the accused.

How to balance those interests is not an easy question.

Maintaining cash bail would minimize some of the risks associated with expansions of pretrial release, because some subset of those detained as a result of their inability to pay would have reoffended. But this is both an inefficient and unjust way to approach mitigating the risks associated with expansions of pretrial release.

In my estimation, a better approach is to structure reforms in such a way that empowers judges to remand dangerous or high-risk offenders to pretrial detention, irrespective of the charges they face. Many presume that the offenses with which a defendant is charged in the instant case are a reliable indicator of the risk that they pose to the public during the pretrial period. They're not. According to a study by the New York City Criminal Justice Agency, "the likelihood of (a failure to appear) and/ or re-arrest for a violent offense was lower among defendants initially arrested for felony-level violent and property offenses" than it was "among defendants initially arrested for all types of misdemeanor or lesser offenses." While this may seem counterintuitive to some, many high-risk offenders often engage in a broad range of misconduct; so, it's not only possible but likely that a high-risk offender will be arrested for what would generally be regarded as a low-level offense.

A fairer and more accurate way for judges to assess a given defendant's risk is through a validated algorithmic risk assessment tool (RAT), which calculates risk based on attaching weights to a variety of factors like criminal history and age. A recent study by the Center for Court Innovation illustrated the predictive accuracy of such a tool—even across racial groups, a crucial criterion, given the opposition of some reformers who claim that racial bias is built into the algorithms. It's worth noting, however, that in New York City, courts have been using an algorithmic RAT to assess flight risk for years—a practice that was left undisturbed by the 2020 reform and the 2021 amendment. Also, in jurisdictions that recently enacted bail reforms (such as New Jersey), the use of RATs hasn't materially changed the racial composition of the jail population. Now, to be clear, it is possible, because of how heavily many RATs weigh criminal history, that an assessment of "erroneous" classifications would reveal that Black defendants (who tend to have more extensive criminal histories compared with white defendants), when misclassified, are more likely to be misclassified as high risk than defendants of other races. Nevertheless, implementing an algorithmic RAT to inform judicial assessments of the dangers that defendants pose to their communities will provide judges with an objective framework to aid them in their pretrial release decisions—one that is far preferable to having them set bail with the hope that dangerous defendants can't come up with the money.

RATs do not have to be the be-all and end-all of the pretrial release decision. Judges should maintain the discretion to consider case-specific evidence that both the prosecution and the defense bring to light, particularly if that evidence can contextualize the risk assessment before them. For example, consider this hypothetical: a defendant who, due to his age and criminal history, scored quite high on an algorithmic RAT was recently paralyzed in a car accident. Judges should probably not be constrained to remand pursuant to the RAT, given the defendant's incapacitating injury. In other words, RATs should be considered highly probative pieces of a bigger body of evidence that ought to be considered in its totality.

Some critics, not unreasonably, highlight the tension between the presumption of innocence and the pretrial detention of a defendant who has not yet been convicted. That tension is very real. However, I would be remiss not to note that the Constitution does not require forbidding the latter to serve the former. Minimizing that tension is a public policy problem that, unlike most policy issues, is almost purely a matter of resource allocation.

Simply put, a better-funded criminal justice system can afford more prosecutors, public defenders, investigators, and judges. This is the most direct route to shortening pretrial detention periods as well as to ensuring that the Constitution's guarantee of a speedy trial is fulfilled in all cases. Notably, the state of New Jersey's bail reform capped the pretrial detention period at 180 days and set aside funding for 20 new superior court judgeships to help move cases along. A real effort to assess how much capacity needs to be added to speed up the resolution of cases is the first step toward a long-term solution to many of the issues surrounding criminal prosecutions. Here is where the federal government may be able to play the role of facilitator by directing funds to states and localities whose criminal justice systems are most severely underfunded so that defendants in those jurisdictions stand to spend as little time in pretrial detention as possible.

Like many public policy issues, bail reform is complex. Those who have supported and pushed for reforms (as well as those who continue to do so) are trying to address real problems worthy of serious consideration and our best efforts. Addressing those problems, however, involves trade-offs and requires a balancing of legitimate concerns about justice with equally legitimate concerns about public safety. While I have tried to propose a better way forward, it should be understood that neither of the two competing concerns at issue in this debate will ever be fully eliminated. After all, opening a door to the pretrial detention of a dangerous defendant does not guarantee that their judge will walk through it, as we've seen from some of the terrible stories out of Chicago, whose bail reform does allow judges to do just that.

My hope is that this statement along with my remarks on February 26 help the commission better understand the issues and interests at stake, and that they provide some support for the approach outlined therein. Thank you.

# NOTES

## INTRODUCTION

1. Jeremy Ross, "Leaked CPD Video Shows Fatal Shooting of Brittany Hill While She Was Holding Her 1-Year-Old Daughter," CBS Chicago, June 2, 2019.

2. Matthew Hendrickson, "Baby Waved, Smiled at Men Right before They Killed Her Mother, Prosecutors Say," *Chicago Sun-Times*, May 30, 2019.

3. Joe Flood, "Why the Bronx Burned," *New York Post*, May 16, 2010.

4. Albert Samaha, "The Rise and Fall of Crime in New York City: A Timeline," *The Village*, August 7, 2014.

5. James Q. Wilson and George L. Kelling, "Broken Windows," *The Atlantic*, March 1982.

6. George L. Kelling and William J. Bratton, "Declining Crime Rates: Insiders' Views of the New York City Story," *Journal of Criminal Law and Criminology* 88, no. 4 (Summer 1998).

7. Chris Coons and Thom Tillis, "America's Criminal Justice System is Broken," CNN, January 9, 2017.

8. Mariame Kaba, "Yes, We Mean Literally Abolish the Police," *New York Times*, June 12, 2020.

9. Bryan Stevenson, "Slavery Gave America a Fear of Black People and a Taste for Violent Punishment. Both Still Define Our Criminal-Justice System," *New York Times Magazine*, August 14, 2019.

10. See, for example, Cody W. Telep and David Weisburd, "Crime Concentrations at Places," *The Oxford Handbook of Environmental Criminology* (Oxford University Press, 2018).

11. See, for example, Rafael A. Mangual, "Sub-Chicago and America's Real Crime Rate," *City Journal* (Summer 2017); and Rafael A. Mangual, "Carnage, Continued," *City Journal* (September 14, 2017).

# CHAPTER 1: CONTEXTUALIZING THE REFORM DEBATE

1. Barry Latzer, *The Rise and Fall of Violent Crime in America* (Encounter Books, 2016).

2. *Floyd, et al. v. City of New York, et al.*, Active Cases, Constitutional Rights, last modified September 1, 2021.

3. Sarah Lawrence, "Court-Ordered Population Caps in California County Jails," Stanford Criminal Justice Center (December 2014).

4. *Brown, et al. v. Plata, et al.*, 563 US 493 (2011).

5. Jim Parsons, Qing Wei, Christian Henrichson, Ernest Drucker, and Jennifer Trone, "End of an Era?" Vera Institute of Justice (January 2015).

6. "Fair Sentencing Act," ACLU.

7. Linda Fairstein, "Netflix's False Story of the Central Park Five," *Wall Street Journal*, June 10, 2019.

8. E. Ann Carson, "Prisoners in 2019," Bureau of Justice Statistics (October 2020).

9. US DOJ, FBI, "About Crime in the U.S.," 2009 (September 2010).

10. US DOJ, FBI, "Crime in the U.S.," 2019, table 29 (2019).

11. US DOJ, FBI, "About Crime in the U.S.," 2009 (September 2010).

12. US DOJ, FBI, "Crime in the U.S.," 2019, table 74 (2019).

13. See for example, Todd D. Minton, Zhen Zeng, and Laura M. Maruschak, "Impact of COVID-19 on the Local Jail Population, January–June 2020," Bureau of Justice Statistics (March 2021).

14. Louise Hall, "AOC Suggests NYC Crime Spike Linked to Unemployment and Parents Shoplifting to Feed Children," *The Independent*, July 13, 2020.

15. See *NYPD Compstat Report*, vol. 27, no. 52 (covering the week of December 21, 2020–December 27, 2020).

16. "Murders in US Very Concentrated: 54% of US Counties in 2014 Had Zero Murders, 2% of Counties Have 51% of the Murders," Crime Prevention Research Center (April 25, 2017).

17. "Murders in US Very Concentrated."

18. United States Department of Justice (US DOJ), Federal Bureau of Investigation (FBI), "Crime in the U.S.," 2019, table 4 (2019).

19. US DOJ, FBI, "Crime in the U.S.," 2019, table 4 (2019).

20. US DOJ, FBI, "Crime in the U.S.," 2019, table 8 (2019).

21. David Weisburd, "The Law of Crime Concentration and the Criminology of Place," *Criminology* 53 (May 2015).

22. A street segment is defined as both sides of a street between two intersections (e.g., both sides of 45th Street between Madison Avenue and Fifth Avenue).

23. See Weisburd, "The Law of Crime Concentration," n. 32.

24. David Weisburd and Taryn Zastrow, "Crime Hot Spots: A Study of New York City Streets in 2010, 2015, and 2020," Manhattan Institute (August 18, 2021).

25. Weisburd and Zastrow, "Crime Hot Spots."

26. "Crime and Enforcement Activity Reports," NYPD.

27. "U.S. Census Bureau QuickFacts," US Census Bureau.

28. "Shooting Video Played at Sentencing," *Chicago Sun-Times*, YouTube, March 9, 2017.

29. Jason Meisner, "Chicago Man Freed from Prison, Given $25 Million. He Spends His Second Chance Rebuilding His Old Gang," *Chicago Tribune*, March 9, 2017.

30. Mark K. Levitan and Susan S. Wieler, "Poverty in New York City, 1969–99: The Influence of Demographic Change, Income Growth, and Income Inequality," *FRBNY Economic Policy Review* (July 2008).

31. "New York City Government Poverty Measure 2005–2016: An Annual Report from the Office of the Mayor," Poverty Research Unit of the Mayor's Office for Economic Opportunity, April 2018.

32. "Only 1 in 4 Young Black Men in New York City Has a Job," Community Service Society, December 10, 2010.

33. Juliana Menasce Horowitz, Ruth Igielnik, and Rakesh Kochhar, "Most Americans Say There Is Too Much Economic Inequality in the U.S., but Fewer Than Half Call It a Top Priority," *Pew Research Center* (January 9, 2020).

34. "Index of Crime: United States, 1981–2000," Census Bureau.

35. US DOJ, FBI, "Crime in the U.S.," 1997–2016, table 1 (2016).

36. "New York City Government Poverty Measure 2005–2016: An Annual Report from the Office of the Mayor," Poverty Research Unit of the Mayor's Office for Economic Opportunity, April 2018.

37. DA Larry Krasner (@DA_LarryKrasner), Twitter thread, 10:44 a.m., June 17, 2019.

38. Steve Keeley (@KeeleyFox29), Twitter tweet, 11:29 a.m., September 26, 2021.

39. See Latzer, *The Rise and Fall*, 50 n. 12.

40. Latzer, *The Rise and Fall*, 50 n. 12.

41. Latzer, *The Rise and Fall*, 50 n. 12.

42. Latzer, *The Rise and Fall*, 145.

43. Latzer, *The Rise and Fall*, 100.

44. Matthew Delisi, John Paul Wright, and Rafael A. Mangual, "Pychology, Not Circumstances: Understanding 'Crime as Entitlement'," *City Journal*, forthcoming.

45. Donald W. Black, "The Natural History of Antisocial Personality Disorder," *Canadian Journal of Psychiatry, Revue Anadienne de Psychiatrie* 60, no. 7 (July 2015): 309–314.

46. M. R. Rautiainen, T. Paunio, E. Repo-Tiihonen, et al., "Genome-Wide Association Study of Antisocial Personality Disorder," *Translational Psychiatry* 6, e883 (2016).

47. "2021 Poverty Guidelines," ASPE, February 2021.

48. Jessica Semega, Melissa Kollar, John Creamer, and Abinash Mohanty, "Income and Poverty in the United States: 2018," US Census Bureau P60-266, September 10, 2019, last revised October 8, 2021.

49. See, for example, Bernadette Rabuy and Daniel Kopf, "Prisons of Poverty: Uncovering the pre-incarceration incomes of the imprisoned," Prison Policy Initiative (July 9, 2015). (Showing that 57 percent of male prisoners had incomes below $22,500, which is almost double the current poverty threshold.)

50. "2019 National Survey of Drug Use and Health (NSDUH) Releases," SAMHSA.

51. Delisi, Wright, and Mangual, "Psychology, Not Circumstances."

52. Marcus Berzofsky, Jennifer Bronson, Jessica Stroop, and Stephanie Zimmer, "Drug, Dependence, and Abuse Among State Prisoners and Jail Inmates, 2007–2009," Bureau of Justice Statistics (June 2017).

53. David Weisburd, Sarit Weisburd, Alese Wooditch, and Sue-Ming Yang, "Do Stop, Question, and Frisk Practices Deter Crime? Evidence at Microunits of Space and Time," *Criminology and Public Policy*, November 2015.

## CHAPTER TWO: AGAINST MASS DECARCERATION, PART 1: POST-CONVICTION INCARCERATION

1. Likipedia, "Seinfeld—Post Office Wanted Posters Carson, 1989," YouTube, September 20, 2017.

2. Jro211, "Richard Pryor: Prison," YouTube, July 23, 2006.

3. Rafael A. Mangual, "Elizabeth Warren's Criminal-Justice Illiteracy," *National Review* (June 19, 2018).

4. Kamala Harris, "Kamala's Plan to Transform the Criminal Justice System and Re-Envision Public Safety in America," Medium, September 9, 2019.

5. Cory Booker, "Pass the Next Step Act," in *Ending Mass Incarceration: Ideas from Today's Leaders*, ed. Inimai Chettiar and Priya Raghavan (Brennan Center for Justice, 2019): 2.

6. Katherine Miller, "Joe Biden Told a Voter He'll 'Go Further" Than Cutting Incarceration by 50%," Buzzfeed News, July 9, 2019; ACLU, "Joe Biden on Criminal Justice in Charleston, SC on 7/7/19," YouTube, July 8, 2019.

7. Linda Kersten et al., "Community Violence Exposure and Conduct Problems in Children and Adolescents with Conduct Disorder and Healthy Controls," *Frontiers in Behavioral Neuroscience* 11 (2019); James Garbarino, Catherine P. Bradshaw, and Joseph A. Vorrasi, "Mitigating the Effects of Gun Violence on Children and Youth," *Future Child* 12, no. 2 (Summer–Fall 2002): 72–85.

8. Patrick T. Sharkey et al., "The Effect of Local Violence on Children's Attention and Impulse Control," *American Journal of Public Health* 102, no. 12 (December 2012): 2287–2293; Patrick Sharkey, "The Acute Effect of Local Homicides on Children's Cognitive Performance," *Proceedings of the National Academy of Sciences* 107, no. 26 (June 2010): 11733–11738.

9. Kamala Harris, "Strengthen Resources for Public Defenders and Hold Prosecutors Accountable," in *Ending Mass Incarceration: Ideas from Today's Leaders*, ed. Inimai Chettiar and Priya Raghavan (Brennan Center for Justice, 2019): 37.

10. See Booker, "Pass the Next Step Act," n. 70.

11. See Booker, "Pass the Next Step Act," n. 70.

12. See Rafael A. Mangual, "The Toxic Narrative about Police Is Wrong," *City Journal*, June 2, 2020, https://www.city-journal.org/toxic-narrative-about-police-is-wrong; Rafael A. Mangual, "Mass Decarceration Is Not the Problem," *Newsweek*, July 29, 2020, https://www.newsweek.com/mass-decarceration-not-answer-opinion-1521488.

13. Floyd Feeney, "German and American Prosecutions: An Approach to Statistical Comparison," US DOJ, Bureau of Justice Statistics (BJS), September 25, 1998, 28.

14. See, for example, Hans-Jörg Albrecht, "Sentencing in Germany: Explaining Long-Term Stability in the Structure of Criminal Sanctions and Sentencing," *Law and Contemporary Problems* 76, no. 211 (2013): 226. (Specifically, see graph 7, p. 226, showing almost no change in both the number of willful homicide convictions and life sentences handed down in willful homicide cases.)

15. "Press Release: Government Targets Illegal Firearms," Home Office and the Rt. Hon. Theresa May MP, February 8, 2012.

16. Danielle Kaeble, "Time Served in State Prison, 2018," US DOJ, BJS, March 2021, tables 1, 2.

17. See Georgina Sturge, "UK Prison Population Statistics," House of Commons Library (October 29, 2021), 11; Carson, "Prisoners in 2019," table 13.

18. Christopher Ingraham, "There Are More Guns Than People in the United States, according to a New Study of Global Firearm Ownership," *Washington Post*, June 19, 2018.

19. Adam Aspinall, "Exclusive: There are 4 Million Guns on UK Streets—and 4,000 Youngsters Have Shotgun Licences," *The Mirror*, March 20, 2016.

20. See "Intentional Homicides (per 100,000 People)—Brazil, United States," UN Office on Drugs and Crime's International Homicide Statistics database (homicide rate comparisons); and "Half of the World's Prison Population of about Nine Million Is Held in the US, China or Russia," BBC News.

21. See Matthew Durose and Patrick Langan, *Felony Sentences in State Courts, 2000*, Bureau of Justice Statistics Bulletin (June 2003); Matthew Durose and Patrick Langan, *Felony Sentences in State Courts, 2002*, Bureau of Justice Statistics Bulletin (December 2004); Matthew Durose and Patrick Langan, *Felony Sentences in State Courts, 2004*, Bureau of Justice Statistics Bulletin (July 2007); and Matthew Durose and Donald Farole, *Felony Sentences in State Courts, 2006*, Bureau of Justice Statistics (December 2009).

22. Carson, "Prisoners in 2019."

23. Carson, "Prisoners in 2019."

24. See Matthew Durose, Alexia Cooper, and Howard Snyder, "Recidivism of Prisoners Released in 30 States in 2005: Patterns from 2005 to 2010," US DOJ, BJS, April 2014, table 5; Leonardo Antenangeli and Matthew Durose, "Recidivism of Prisoners Released in 24 States in 2008: A 10-Year Follow-Up (2008–2018)," US DOJ, BJS, September 2021, table 3; Matthew Durose and Leonardo Antenangeli, "Recidivism of Prisoners Released in 34 States in 2012: A 5-Year Follow-Up Period (2012–2017)," US DOJ, BJS, July 2021, table 3.

25. John J. Dilulio Jr., "The Numbers Don't Lie: It's the Hard Core Doing Hard Time," Brookings Institution, March 17, 1996.

26. Carson, "Prisoners in 2019," table 13.

27. See Mark Motivans, "Federal Justice Statistics, 2017–2018," US DOJ, BJS, April 2021, 10.

28. See, for example, "Research Summary: Plea and Charge Bargaining," US DOJ, Bureau of Justice Assistance (BJA), January 2011.

29. Danielle Kaeble, "Time Served in State Prison, 2018," US DOJ, BJS, March 2021, table 1.

30. Kaeble, "Time Served in State Prison, 2018," table 2.

31. Kaeble, "Time Served in State Prison, 2018," table 2.

32. Kaeble, "Time Served in State Prison, 2018," table 2, highlights on page 1.

33. Timothy Hughes and Doris James Wilson, "Reentry Trends in the United States," US DOJ, October 2002.

34. Mariel Alpher, Matthew Durose, and Joshua Markman, "2018 Update on Prisoner Recidivism: A 9-Year Follow-up Period (2005–2014)," US DOJ, BJS, May 2018, 2005 cohort.

35. Antenangeli and Durose, "Recidivism of Prisoners Released in 24 States in 2008," table 4.

36. Antenangeli and Durose, "Recidivism of Prisoners Released in 24 States in 2008," table 4.

37. Antenangeli and Durose, "Recidivism of Prisoners Released in 24 States in 2008," table 4.

38. Alpher, Durose, and Markman, "2018 Update on Prisoner Recidivism," table 7.

39. Antenangeli and Durose, "Recidivism of Prisoners Released in 24 States in 2008," table 10; Alpher, Durose, and Markman, "2018 Update on Prisoner Recidivism," table 7.

40. Antenangeli and Durose, "Recidivism of Prisoners Released in 24 States in 2008," table 9.

41. "Recidivism among Federal Offenders: A Comprehensive Overview," United States Sentencing Commission (March 2016): 5.

42. "Recidivism among Federal Offenders," 20.

43. "Recidivism among Federal Firearms Offenders," United States Sentencing Commission (June 2019): 4.

44. Carson, "Prisoners in 2019," table 15.

45. Rachel E. Morgan and Alexandra Thompson, "Criminal Victimization, 2020," US DOJ, BJS, October 2020, 1.

46. US DOJ, FBI, "Crime in the U.S. (2019)," table 25.

47. See, for example, Dana Goldstein, "How to Cut the Prison Population by 50 Percent," Marshall Project (March 4, 2015); Van Jones, "Cut 50 Percent of the Prison Population," in *Ending Mass Incarceration: Ideas from Today's Leaders*, ed. Inimai Chettiar and Priya Raghavan (Brennan Center for Justice, 2019), 49; James Austin, Lauren-Brooke Eisen, James Cullen, and Jonathan Frank, "How Many Americans are Unnecessarily Incarcerated?" Brennan Center for Justice, 2016.

48. James Q. Wilson, *Thinking about Crime*, 142.

49. See Alpher, Durose, and Markman, "2018 Update on Prisoner Recidivism," highlights on page 1; Antenangeli and Durose, "Recidivism of Prisoners Released in 24 States in 2008," highlights on page 1.

50. See Antenangeli and Durose, "Recidivism of Prisoners Released in 24 States in 2008," table 11; Alpher, Durose, and Markman, "2018 Update on Prisoner Recidivism," table 7.

51. Kevin Rector, "2017 Homicide Data Provide Insight into Baltimore's Gun Wars, Police Say," *Baltimore Sun*, January 3, 2018.

52. Wilson, *Thinking about Crime*, 142.

53. Wilson, *Thinking about Crime*, 141–142.

54. Wilson, *Thinking about Crime*, 142–143. Wilson highlighted two studies done by researchers at the Rand Corporation and at INSLAW, which identified high-rate offenders and "career criminals" with reasonable accuracy—studies he hoped could be improved on with further research.

55. See Brian A. Reaves, "Violent Felons in Large Urban Counties," BJS Special Report (July 2006).

56. See Rector, "2017 Homicide Data Provide Insight," n. 115.

57. "Gun Violence in Chicago, 2016," University of Chicago Crime Lab, January 2017, 16.

58. See Ryan S. King, Marc Mauer, and Malcom C. Young, "Incarceration and Crime: A Complex Relationship," Sentencing Project, 2005, citing William Spelman, "The Limited Importance of Prison Expansion," in *The Crime Drop in America*, Alfred Blumstein and Joel Wallman, eds. (Cambridge University Press, 2000), 97–129.

59. Patrick Sharkey, *Uneasy Peace*, 49.

60. Eric Helland and Alexander Tabarrok, "Does Three Strikes Deter? A Non-Parametric Estimation," 2007.

61. See Rachel E. Barkow, *Prisoners of Politics: Breaking the Cycle of Mass Incarceration* at page 3.

62. Barkow, *Prisoners of Politics*, 205.

63. Charles E. Loeffler and Daniel S. Nagin, "The Impact of Recidivism," *Annual Review of Criminology* 5, no. 1 (2022).

64. Loeffler and Daniel S. Nagin, "The Impact of Recidivism."

65. Ta-Nehisi Coates, "The Black Family in the Age of Mass Incarceration," *The Atlantic*, October 2015.

66. Coates, "The Black Family in the Age of Mass Incarceration."

67. "The Endless Catastrophe of Rikers Island," *New York Times*, September 15, 2021.

68. "Pretrial Criminal Justice Research," Laura and John Arnold Foundation, November 2013.

## CHAPTER THREE: AGAINST MASS DECARCERATION, PART 2: PRETRIAL DETENTION

1. Wendy Sawyer and Peter Wagner, "Mass Incarceration: The Whole Pie 2020," Prison Policy Initiative, March 24, 2020.

2. Bryan A. Garner, ed., *Black's Law Dictionary*, 9th ed. (West, 2009), 160.

3. A bail bond is essentially a guarantee to return the defendant to court made by a defendant's surety, backed by the surety's assumption of financial liability to the court should the defendant fail to appear. See Garner, *Black's Law Dictionary*, 200.

4. See, for example, "Addressing the Poverty Penalty and Bail Reform," Fair and Just Prosecution: "The money bail system . . . often means that wealthier defendants get released while poor defendants have to stay in jail"; "Moving Beyond Money: A Primer on Bail Reform," Criminal Justice Policy Program at Harvard Law School, October 2016: "The core critique of money bail is that it causes individuals to be jailed simply because they lack the financial means to post a bail payment."

5. See "Jail: Who Is in on Bail?" New York City Mayor's Office of Criminal Justice, May 2019.

NOTES

6. See Rafael A. Mangual, "Reforming New York's Bail Reform: A Public Safety-Minded Proposal," Manhattan Institute, Issue Brief (March 2020): 6–8.

7. Will Dobbie, Jacob Goldin, and Crystal Yang, "The Effects of Pre-Trial Detention on Conviction, Future Crime, and Employment: Evidence from Randomly Assigned Judges," *American Economic Review* 108, no. 2 (February 2018).

8. Paul Cassell and Richard Fowles, "Does Bail Reform Increase Crime? An Empirical Assessment of the Public Safety Implications of Bail Reform in Cook County, Illinois," Utah Law Faculty Scholarship (2020), 194.

9. Don Stemen and David Olson, "Dollars and Sense in Cook County: Examining the Impact of General Order 18.8A on Felony Bond Court Decisions, Pretrial Release, and Crime," Safety and Justice Challenge Research Consortium (November 2020).

10. Charles F. Lehman, "Yes, Bail Reform in Chicago Has Increased Crime," *City Journal* (February 10, 2021).

11. Brian A. Reaves, "Violent Felons in Large Urban Counties, State Court Processing Statistics, 1990–2002," Bureau of Justice Statistics (July 2006): 1.

12. Edgar Sandoval, "A Teenager Went 3 Floors Down to Play Video Games. He Never Came Home," *New York Times*, January 21, 2021.

13. See, for example, Graham Raymon and Thomas Tracy, "Cops Arrest Man Who Set Up Shooting That Killed Innocent NYC Teen; Victim's Brother Separately Charged with Gun Possession," *New York Daily News*, January 15, 2021.

14. See Rocco Parascandola and Thomas Tracy, "Suspect Busted in Brooklyn Subway Station Assault Was Freed through State's New Bail Reform Laws," *New York Daily News,* February 2, 2020.

15. See Qudsia Siddiqi, "Predicting the Likelihood of Pretrial Failure to Appear and/or Re-Arrest for a Violent Offense among New York City Defendants: An Analysis of the 2001 Dataset," New York City Criminal Justice Agency (January 2009).

16. George Kelling, "Community Policing, Rightly Understood," *City Journal* (Winter 2019).

17. See Sarah Picard et al., *Beyond the Algorithm: Pretrial Reform, Risk Assessment, and Racial Fairness*, Center for Court Innovation (July 2019).

18. Two illustrations of "erroneous" classifications would be if a defendant classified as low risk is rearrested during the observation period, and if a defendant classified as high risk makes it through the observation period without being

rearrested. With respect to the latter, it is important to keep in mind that the absence of an arrest does not necessarily mean that the defendant did not reoffend, given the reality that many offenses go unreported or do not result in arrest due to lack of detection.

19. See Picard et al., *Beyond the Algorithm*, n. 149.

20. See, for example, *U.S. v. Salerno*, 481 U.S. 739 (1987) (holding that the presumption of innocence is not violated by a defendant's pretrial detention on public safety grounds).

21. Glenn A. Grant, "Criminal Justice Reform Report to the Governor and the Legislature for Calendar Year 2017," New Jersey Judiciary, February 2018.

## CHAPTER FOUR: THE MORE COMPLICATED STORY OF INCARCERATION AND THE FAMILY

1. "The Economics and Politics of Race," Firing Line broadcast records, Hoover Institution Library and Archives, November 3, 1983, at 06:18.

2. Jeremy Travis, *Perspectives on Crime and Justice*, 109.

3. Van Jones, "Cut 50 Percent of the Prison Population," 49.

4. Van Jones, "Cut 50 Percent of the Prison Population," 49.

5. See, for example, Elizabeth Weill-Greenberg, "'It Tears Families Apart': Lawmakers Nationwide Are Moving to End Mandatory Sentencing," *The Appeal*, April 15, 2021.

6. Elizabeth Warren, "Rethinking Public Safety to Reduce Mass Incarceration and Strengthen Communities," Team Warren (blog), Medium, August 20, 2019, https://medium.com/@teamwarren/rethinking-public-safety-to-reduce-mass-incarceration-and-strengthen-communities-90e8591c6255.

7. "The Biden Plan for Strengthening America's Commitment to Justice," Joebiden.com, accessed January 10, 2022, https://joebiden.com/justice.

8. Bernie Sanders, "Justice and Safety for All," Bernie Sanders official website, accessed January 10, 2022, https://berniesanders.com/issues/criminal-justice-reform.

9. Mike Lee, "The Conservative Case for Criminal Justice Reform," *The Federalist*, October 7, 2015.

10. Lee, "The Conservative Case for Criminal Justice Reform."

11. Arthur L. Rizer III, "The Conservative Case for Jail Reform," *National Affairs*, no. 33 (Fall 2017).

12. While the federal government does plenty (often too much) to create and enforce criminal laws, this particular part of the book is focused on the question of incarceration, which is still mostly a function of state law. Indeed, state prisons house about 88 percent of US prisoners—that's according to data through 2019. See generally Carson, "Prisoners in 2019," 108.

13. Eric Gonzalez, "Justice 2020: An Action Plan for Brooklyn," Brooklyn District Attorney's Office, March 11, 2019, 5.

14. Bruce Golding, Larry Celona, and Reuven Fenton. "Convicted Killer Released without Bail by Judge with Political Connections." *New York Post*, October 23, 2019.

15. Golding, Celona, and Fenton, "Convicted Killer Released."

16. Rebekah Levine Coley, Jennifer Carrano, and Selva Lewin-Bizan, "Unpacking Links between Fathers' Antisocial Behaviors and Children's Behavior Problems: Direct, Indirect, and Interactive Effects." *Journal of Abnormal Child Psychology* 39, no. 6 (August 2011): 791–804.

17. Coley, Carrano, and Lewin-Bizan, "Unpacking Links."

18. Sara R. Jaffee et al., "Life with (or without) Father: The Benefits of Living with Two Biological Parents Depend on the Father's Antisocial Behavior," *Child Development* 74, no. 1 (February 2003): 109–126.

19. Jaffee et al., "Life with (or without) Father."

20. Jaffee et al., "Life with (or without) Father."

21. Zachary D. Torry and Stephen B. Billick, "Implications of Antisocial Parents," *Psychiatric Quarterly* 82, no. 4 (December 1, 2011): 275–285.

22. Rebecca Walleret al., "Parenting Is an Environmental Predictor of Callous-Unemotional Traits and Aggression: A Monozygotic Twin Differences Study," *Journal of the American Academy of Child and Adolescent Psychiatry* 57, no. 12 (December 1, 2018): 955–963.

23. Elizabeth A. Stormshak et al., "Parenting Practices and Child Disruptive Behavior Problems in Early Elementary School," *Journal of Clinical Child Psychology* 29, no. 1 (2010): 17–29.

24. Stormshak et al., "Parenting Practices and Child Disruptive Behavior Problems."

25. Stormshak et al., "Parenting Practices and Child Disruptive Behavior Problems."

26. See "3 Family Members Charged In Disneyland Brawl Caught on Video," CBS Los Angeles, July 23, 2019; Tracy Bloom, "Man Sentenced to 180 Days in Jail

for Caught-on-Video Fight at Disneyland's Toontown," KTLA NewsNow Las Vegas, February 28, 2020.

27. Seena Fazel and John Danesh, "Serious Mental Disorder in 23000 Prisoners: A Systematic Review of 62 Surveys," *The Lancet* 359, no. 9306 (February 16, 2002): 545–550.

28. Fazel and Danesh, "Serious Mental Disorder in 23000 Prisoners."

29. M-R. Rautiainen et al., "Genome-Wide Association Study of Antisocial Personality Disorder," *Translational Psychiatry* 6, no. 9 (September 2016): e883–e883.

30. Donald W. Black et al., "Antisocial Personality Disorder in Incarcerated Offenders: Psychiatric Comorbidity and Quality of Life," *Annals of Clinical Psychiatry* 22, no. 2 (May 2010): 113–120.

31. Natalia Calvo et al., "Study of Prevalence of Personality Disorders in Inmate Men Sample with Substance Use Disorders Using of PDQ-4+ Self-Report," *Actas Espanolas ee Psiquiatria* 44, no. 5 (September 2016): 178–182.

32. L. J. Warren et al., "Threats to Kill: A Follow-Up Study," *Psychological Medicine* 38, no. 4 (April 2008): 599–605.

33. Tija Zarković Palijan et al., "Relationship between Comorbidity and Violence Risk Assessment in Forensic Psychiatry—the Implication of Neuroimaging Studies," *Psychiatria Danubina* 22, no. 2 (June 2010): 253–256.

34. "Every 25 Seconds: The Human Toll of Criminalizing Drug Use in the United States," Human Rights Watch, October 12, 2016, https://www.hrw.org/report/2016/10/12/every-25-seconds/ human-toll-criminalizing-drug-use-united-states.

35. "Every 25 Seconds."

36. Stephen B. Billings, "Parental Arrest and Incarceration: How Does It Impact the Children?" SSRN Scholarly Paper (Social Science Research Network, May 31, 2018), https://doi.org/10.2139/ssrn.3034539.

37. Manudeep Bhuller et al., "Incarceration Spillovers in Criminal and Family Networks," NBER Working Paper 24878 (National Bureau of Economic Research, August 2018), https://doi.org/10.3386/w24878.

38. Carolina Arteaga, "Parental Incarceration and Children's Educational Attainment," *Review of Economics and Statistics*, October 15, 2021, 1–45, https://doi.org/10.1162/rest_a_01129.

39. Henderson Police Department, "HPD 10.21.19 4th OIS Body Worn Camera," YouTube, November 7, 2019, https://www.youtube.com/watch?v=j61zPopB6gw.

40. *Report on Use of Force: Legal Analysis Surrounding the Death of Claudia Rodriguez-Mendez on October 21, 2019,* Office of Clark County District Attorney, https://files.clarkcountynv.gov/clarknv/Legal%20Analysis%20 Surrounding%20the%20death%20of%20Claudia%20Rodriguez-Mendez%20 on%20October%2021,%202019.pdf.

41. Amy Abdelsayed et al., "UPDATE: Henderson Police Release 911 Call, Body Camera Footage of Shooting Involving Department," KTNV Las Vegas, October 21, 2019.

## CHAPTER FIVE: USE OF FORCE AND THE PRACTICAL LIMITS OF POPULAR POLICE REFORMS

1. Steve Eder, Michael H. Keller, and Blacki Migliozzi, "As New Police Reform Laws Sweep across the U.S., Some Ask: Are They Enough?" *New York Times,* April 18, 2021.

2. David Schuman, "Mpls. City Council Votes Unanimously to Dismantle MPD," CBS Minnesota, June 26, 2020.

3. Rafael A. Mangual, "From Bad to Worse in New York," *City Journal Online,* March 26, 2021.

4. Tina Moore and Craig McCarthy, "NYC's Controversial 'Diaphragm Law' Rejected as 'Unconstitutionally Vague,'" *New York Post,* June 22, 2021.

5. "Fatal Force: Police Shootings Database," *Washington Post.*

6. "Fatal Force: Police Shootings Database," *Washington Post.*

7. The article (including a breakdown of the numbers in Appendix A) can be found here: Rafael A. Mangual, "Police Use of Force and the Practical Limits of Popular Reform Proposals: A Response to Rizer and Mooney," *Federalist Society Review* 21 (May 2020): 128–135. The data (published by department), which may have been updated since the article was published, can be found here: "Get the Data: Explore Data on All Police Shootings from the Nation's 50 Largest Local Police Departments," *Vice News,* December 10, 2017.

8. Federal Bureau of Investigation, *Crime in the United States,* 2018, Table 74 (Full-Time Law Enforcement Employees). Note: This number may undercount the total number of law enforcement officers operating within the US, given that in some parts of the country—particularly in rural, exurban, and some suburban areas—some public safety departments use part-time and/or reserve officers.

9. Federal Bureau of Investigation, *Crime in the United States,* 2018, Table 29 (Estimated Number of Arrests).

10. Erika Harrell and Elizabeth Davis, *Contacts between Police and the Public, 2018—Statistical Tables*, Bureau of Justice Statistics, https://bjs.ojp.gov/content/pub/pdf/cbpp18st.pdf.

11. Dave McMenamin, "LeBron James Says Black Community 'Terrified' of Police Conduct," ESPN, August 25, 2020.

12. American Civil Liberties Union, "The Other Epidemic: Fatal Police Shootings in the Time of Covid-19," ACLU Research Report, 2020.

13. Harrell and Davis, *Contacts between Police and the Public, 2018*, Table 4.

14. Harrell and Davis, *Contacts between Police and the Public, 2018*, Table 4.

15. Shelley Hyland, Lynn Langton, and Elizabeth Davis, *Police Use of Nonfatal Force, 2002–11*, Bureau of Justice Statistics, November 2015, https://www.bjs.gov/content/pub/pdf/punf0211.pdf.

16. William P. Bozeman et al., "Injuries Associated with Police Use of Force," *Journal of Trauma and Acute Care Surgery* 84, no. 3 (March 2018): 466–472.

17. Matthew J. Hickman, *Citizen Complaints about Police Use of Force*, Bureau of Justice Statistics, June 2006.

18. See New York Civilian Complaint Review Board, *Annual Report, 2018*, Figure 52, https://www1.nyc.gov/assets/ccrb/downloads/pdf/policy_pdf/annual_bi-annual/2018CCRB_AnnualReport.pdf.

19. See NYC Mayor's Office of Criminal Justice, *Data Stories*, individual charts for felony arrests and misdemeanors, https://criminaljustice.cityofnewyork.us/data_stories.

20. See "Precision," Contrôle Officiel Suisse des Chronomètres, https://www.cosc.swiss/en/quality/precision.

21. See Jonathan Klick and Alexander Tabarrok, "Using Terror Alert Levels to Estimate the Effect of Police on Crime," *Journal of Law and Economics* 48, no. 1 (April 1, 2005): 267–279.

22. See John M. MacDonald, Jonathan Klick, and Ben Grunwald, "The Effect of Private Police on Crime: Evidence from a Geographic Regression Discontinuity Design," *Journal of the Royal Statistical Society*: Series A (Statistics in Society) 179, part 3 (June 2016): 831–846.

23. See Aaron Chalfin and Justin McCrary, "Are U.S. Cities Underpoliced? Theory and Evidence," *Review of Economics and Statistics* 100, no. 1 (March 2018): 167–186.

24. Aaron Chalfin et al., "Police Force Size and Civilian Race," NBER Working Paper 28202, December 2020, https://www.nber.org/papers/w28202.

25. Tanaya Devi and Roland G. Fryer Jr., "Policing the Police: The Impact of 'Pattern-or-Practice' Investigations on Crime," NBER Working Paper 27324, June 2020, https://www.nber.org/papers/w27324.

26. Barbara Campbell and Suzanne Nuyen, "No-Knock Warrants Banned In Louisville in Law Named for Breonna Taylor," NPR, June 11, 2020.

27. David A. Klinger and Jeff Rojek, "Multi-Method Study of Special Weapons and Tactics Teams, 1986–1998," Sponsored by US DOJ, National Institute of Justice, NCJ no. 223855, January 2005, https://www.ojp.gov/pdffiles1/nij/grants/223855.pdf.

28. New York Police Department, Use of Force Data Tables, https://www1.nyc.gov/site/nypd/stats/reports-analysis/use-of-force-data.page.

29. See Chicago Police Department, *2018 Annual Report*, July 2019, 78–79, http://home.chicagopolice.org/wp-content/uploads/2019/07/2018AnnualReport-05July19.pdf.

30. Chicago Police Department, *2018 Annual Report*, 82.

31. American Civil Liberties Union, "War Comes Home: The Excessive Militarization of American Police," June 2014, https://www.aclu.org/report/war-comes-home-excessive-militarization-american-police.

32. Radley Balko, "The Militarization of America's Police Forces," *Cato's Letter* 11, no. 4 (Fall 2013).

33. See New York Police Department, Annual Use of Force/Firearms Discharge Report Data Tables, https://www1.nyc.gov/site/nypd/stats/reports-analysis/firearms-discharge.page (specifically, see the 2016 data table, which provides annual shooting numbers going back to 1971).

34. New York Police Department, *Use of Force Report, 2019*, 26, https://www1.nyc.gov/assets/nypd/downloads/pdf/use-of-force/use-of-force-2019-2020-11-03.pdf.

35. William A. Geller and Kevin J. Karales, "Shootings of and by Chicago Police: Uncommon Crises—Part I: Shootings by Chicago Police," *Journal of Criminal Law and Criminology* 72, no. 4 (Winter 1981): 1813, 1832.

36. Chicago Police Department, *2019 Annual Report*, September 2020, https://home.chicagopolice.org/wp-content/uploads/2020/09/19AR.pdf.

37. Jon Regardie, "A Deep Dive in to the LAPD's Use of Force Statistics," *Los Angeles Magazine,* June 16, 2020.

38. Arezou Rezvani et al., "MRAPs and Bayonets: What We Know about the Pentagon's 1033 Program," NPR, September 1, 2014.

39. See Casey Delehanty et al., "Militarization and Police Violence: The case of the 1033 Program," *Research and Politics* 4, no. 2 (April 2017).

40. Olugbenga Ajilore, "Is There a 1033 Effect? Police Militarization and Aggressive Policing," MRPA Paper, October 30, 2017, https://mpra.ub.uni-muenchen. de/82543/1/MPRA_.

41. Matthew C. Harris et al., "Peacekeeping Force: Effects of Providing Tactical Equipment to Local Law Enforcement," *American Economic Journal: Economic Policy* 9, no. 3 (2017): 291–313.

42. Vincenzo Bove and Evelina Gavrilova, "Police Officer on the Frontline or a Soldier? The Effect of Police Militarization on Crime," *American Economic Journal: Economic Policy* 9, no. 3 (2017): 1–18.

43. Dara Lind, "Cops Do 20,000 No-Knock Raids a Year. Civilians Often Pay the Price When They Go Wrong," *Vox*, May 15, 2015.

44. Mary Louise Kelly, interview with Radley Balko, "No-Knock Warrants: How Common They Are and Why Police Are Using Them," *All Things Considered*, podcast transcript, NPR, June 12, 2020, https://www.npr.org/2020/06/12/876293168/ no-knock-warrants-how-common-they-are-and-why-police-are-using-them.

45. Kim Parker et al., "The Demographics of Gun Ownership," Pew Research Center, June 22, 2017, https://www.pewresearch.org/social-trends/2017/06/22/ the-demographics-of-gun-ownership.

46. Alison Lynn and Matt Gutman, "Family of Toddler Injured by SWAT 'Grenade' Faces $1M in Medical Bills," ABC News, December 18, 2014.

47. Madeleine Carlisle, "'This Is about True Reparations.' Rep. Ayanna Pressley on the Movement to Defund Police," *Time*, June 25, 2020.

48. Jacob Knutson, "Pew Poll: Americans Support Allowing Citizens to Sue Officers for Misconduct," *Axios*, July 9, 2020.

49. Keith Coffman, "Colorado Reform Law Ends Immunity for Police in Civil Misconduct Cases," Reuters, June 20, 2020.

50. Daniele Selby, "New Mexico Is the Second State to Ban Qualified Immunity," Innocence Project, April 7, 2021.

51. James Craven, "New York City Council Passes Qualified Immunity Reform," Cato at Liberty, Cato Institute, March 31, 2021.

52. Spencer Bokat-Lindell, "The One Police Reform That Both the Left and the Right Support," *New York Times*, June 2, 2020.

53. Radley Balko, "Opinion: The No-Knock Warrant for Breonna Taylor Was Illegal," *Washington Post*, June 3, 2020.

54. Rukmini Callimachi, "Breonna Taylor's Family to Receive $12 Million Settlement from City of Louisville," *New York Times*, October 2, 2020.

55. Steve Karnowski and Amy Forliti, "Floyd Family Agrees to $27M Settlement amidst Ex-Cop's Trial," AP News, March 12, 2021.

56. US Congress, House, *George Floyd Justice in Policing Act of 2020*, HR 7120, 116th Congress, passed in House June 25, 2020, https://www.congress.gov/bill/116th-congress/house-bill/7120.

57. "End the Court Doctrine That Enables Police Brutality," *New York Times*, May 22, 2021.

58. See Seth Mydans, "Rodney King Is Awarded $3.8 Million," *New York Times*, April 20, 1994; "$1 Million per Shot—How Laquan McDonald Settlement Unfolded after That Initial Demand," *Chicago Sun-Times*, June 24, 2016; Neil Vigdor, "Stephon Clark's Sons Reach $2.4 Million Settlement over Police Killing," *New York Times*, October 10, 2019; Vanessa Romo, "New York City Reaches $3.3 Million Settlement with Kalief Browder's Family," NPR, January 25, 2019; Eric Heisig, "Tamir Rice Estate's Multi-Million Dollar Settlement Approved by Probate Court," Cleveland.com, January 11, 2019; Mitch Smith, "Philando Castile Family Reaches $3 Million Settlement," *New York Times*, June 26, 2017; Keith L. Alexander, "Baltimore Reaches $6.4 Million Settlement with Freddie Gray's Family," *Washington Post*, September 8, 2015; J. David Goodman, "Eric Garner Case Is Settled by New York City for $5.9 Million," *New York Times*, July 14, 2015; "Michael Brown's Family Received $1.5 Million Settlement with Ferguson," NBC News, June 23, 2017.

59. CAPstat, NYC Federal Civil Rights Lawsuit Data, 2015 to June 2018, https://www.capstat.nyc.

60. See CAPstat, Lawsuits against New York City Police Officers, https://www.capstat.nyc/lawsuits/?page=80&causes_of_action__value=&charge_group__value=&penal_charges__value=&charge_outcomes__value=&stop_location__value=&county__value=&plaintiff_race__value=&plaintiff_gender__value=&attorney_fees=&outcome=&settlement_amount=&tags__value=&incident_date=&force_details__value=&sort=-settlement_amount (showing nine verdicts for the defense, eighteen grants of summary judgement to the defense, thirty-one dismissals with prejudice, and sixteen dismissals without prejudice).

61. Joanna C. Schwartz, "How Qualified Immunity Fails," *Yale Law Journal* 127, no. 1 (October 2017).

62. Joanna C. Schwartz, "Qualified Immunity's Selection Effects," *Northwestern University Law Review* 114, no. 5 (March 2020).

63. Joanna C. Schwartz, "Police Indemnification," *New York University Law Review* 89, no. 3 (June 2014).

64. *Saucier v. Katz,* 533 US 194 (2001), https://supreme.justia.com/cases/federal/us/533/194.

65. *Pearson v. Callahan*, 555 US 223 (2009).

66. Charles Fain Lehman, "Policing without the Police? A Review of the Evidence," Manhattan Institute, April 21, 2021, https://www.manhattan-institute.org/policing-without-police-review-evidence.

67. Jerry H. Ratcliffe, "Policing and Public Health Calls for Service in Philadelphia," *Crime Science* 10, no. 5.

68. Greg B. Smith, "The NYPD's Mental Illness Response Breakdown," *The City*, March 21, 2019.

69. Health Resources and Services Administration, National Center for Health Workforce Analysis; Substance Abuse and Mental Health Services Administration, Office of Policy, Planning, and Innovation, *National Projections of Supply and Demand for Selected Behavioral Health Practitioners: 2013–2025,* November 2016, https://bhw.hrsa.gov/sites/default/files/bureau-health-workforce/data-research/behavioral-health-2013-2025.pdf.

70. See US DOJ, *Law Enforcement Best Practices: Lessons Learned from the Field,* 27, Office of Community Oriented Policing Services (2019), https://cops.usdoj.gov/RIC/Publications/cops-w0875-pub.pdf (citing Len Bowers, "A Model of De-Escalation," *Mental Health Practice* 17, no. 9 (June 2014), https://www.deepdyve.com/lp/royal-college-of-nursing-rcn/a-model-of-de-escalation-1tglcwO9E0).

71. US DOJ, *Law Enforcement Best Practices.*

72. US DOJ, *Law Enforcement Best Practices.*

73. US DOJ, *Law Enforcement Best Practices*, 27. "[M]uch of what we know about de-escalation comes from the empirical literature of clinicians. These practitioners were—just as law enforcement agencies are today—looking to reduce the instances of violent or otherwise disruptive behaviors in healthcare settings" (internal citations omitted).

74. See Owen Price et al., "Learning and Performance Outcomes of Mental Health Staff Training in De-escalation Techniques for the Management of Violence and Aggression," *British Journal of Psychiatry* 206, no. 6 (June 2015): 447–455.

75. Price et al., "Learning and Performance Outcomes."

76. Michael S. Rogers, Dale E. McNiel, and Renée L. Binder, "Effectiveness of Police Crisis Intervention Training Programs," *Journal of the American Academy of Psychiatry and the Law* 47, no. 4 (2019).

77. Robin S. Engel et al., "Does De-escalation Training Work? A Systematic Review and Call for Evidence in Police Use-of-Force Reform," *Criminology and Public Policy* 19, no. 3 (August 2020): 721–759. It is worth noting that Engel is the author of a more recent study showing promising results of a de-escalation training program developed by the Police Executive Research Forum, highlighting an important justification for the continued pursuit of workable reforms, even if early results suggest disappointing outcomes (see Robin S. Engel et al., "Assessing the Impact of De-escalation Training on Police Behavior: Reducing Police Use of Force in the Louisville, KY Metro Police Department," *Criminology and Public Policy*, January 12, 2022).

78. Los Angeles Police Department, "Van Nuys Area Officer Involved Shooting 12/31/18," YouTube, February 14, 2019, https://www.youtube.com/watch?v=bI4qB66UY10.

## CHAPTER SIX: THE OTHER SIDE OF THE "FALSE-POSITIVE PROBLEM"

1. James R. Copland, "In Policing, Race Matters," *National Review*, August 20, 2020.

2. John McWhorter, *Authentically Black: Essays for the Black Silent Majority* (Gotham Books, 2003), 38.

3. "Ending Racist Stop and Frisk," ACLU Massachusetts, https://www.aclum.org/en/ending-racist-stop-and-frisk#learn.

4. Radley Balko, "There's Overwhelming Evidence That the Criminal Justice System Is Racist. Here's the Proof," *Washington Post*, June 10, 2020.

5. Elijah Anderson, *Code of the Street: Decency, Violence, and the Moral Life of the Inner City* (W. W. Norton, 1999), 17.

6. Louis Nelson, "Sen. Tim Scott Reveals Incidents of Being Targeted by Capitol Police," Politico, July 13, 2016.

7. Richard Pryor, *Richard Pryor: Live in Concert,* directed by Jeff Margolis (Long Beach, CA: Elkins Entertainment, 1979), streaming on Netflix, https://www.netflix.com/title/907090.

8. Cedric the Entertainer, "Cedric the Entertainer 'We Wish' 'Kings of Comedy,'" Walter Latham Comedy, YouTube Video, August 11, 2011, https://www.youtube.com/watch?v=o5osw5u9Uq4.

9. Chuck Vinson, director, "Blood Is Thicker Than Mud," *The Fresh Prince of Bel-Air*, season 4, episode 8 (NBC Productions, 1993), https://www.youtube.com/watch?v=EXmx3GhYfX4.

10. Rae Kraus, director, "72 Hours," *The Fresh Prince of Bel-Air*, season 1, episode 23 (NBC Productions, 1991), https://www.youtube.com/watch?v=IPeDAFTgPTA.

11. Slaughterhouse, "Slaughterhouse—R.N.S.," YouTube video, July 20, 2015, https://www.youtube.com/watch?v=UNRdr1w3rBs.

12. Anderson, *Code of the Street*, 20 n. 277.

13. Dave Chappelle, *Dave Chappelle: Equanimity*, directed by Stan Lathan (Netflix Studios, 2017), streaming on Netflix.

14. Anderson, *Code of the Street*, 22 n. 277.

15. Anderson, *Code of the Street*, 22 n. 277.

16. Anderson, *Code of the Street*, 29.

17. Trey Ellis, "How Does It Feel to Be a Problem?" in *Speak My Name: Black Men on Masculinity and the American Dream*, ed. Don Belton (Boston: Beacon Press, 1997).

18. Eric A Stewart and Ronald L. Simons, "Race, Code of the Street, and Violent Delinquency: A Multilevel Investigation of Neighborhood Street Culture and Individual Norms of Violence," *Criminology* 48, no. 2 (May 2010): 569–605.

19. Erving Goffman, *The Presentation of Self in Everyday Life* (Anchor, 1959).

20. Goffman, *The Presentation of Self in Everyday Life*, 6.

21. Goffman, *The Presentation of Self in Everyday Life*, 4.

22. Goffman, *The Presentation of Self in Everyday Life*, 13.

23. Goffman, *The Presentation of Self in Everyday Life*, 13.

24. See McWhorter, *Authentically Black*, 57–58 n. 274.

25. Joshua Correll et al., "The Police Officer's Dilemma: A Decade of Research on Racial Bias in the Decision to Shoot," *Social and Personality Psychology Compass* 8, no. 5 (May 2014): 201–213.

26. Jessica J. Sim, Joshua Correll, and Melody S. Sadler, "Understanding Police and Expert Performance: When Training Attenuates (vs. Exacerbates) Stereotypic

Bias in the Decision to Shoot," *Personality and Social Psychology Bulletin* 39, no. 3 (March 2013): 291–304.

27. Roland G. Fryer Jr., "An Empirical Analysis of Racial Differences in Police Use of Force," *Journal of Political Economy* 127, no. 3 (June 2019).

28. "Stop and Frisk in the de Blasio Era," New York Civil Liberties Union, March 2019, https://www.nyclu.org/en/publications/stop-and-frisk-de-blasio-era-2019.

29. This is excluding Staten Island, which created a new precinct in 2013, drastically reconfiguring the boundaries of two of the borough's three precincts at the time, and the Central Park precinct, which has virtually no residents.

30. NYC Crime Map, City of New York, https://maps.nyc.gov/crime.

31. New York Police Department, "Seven Major Felony Offenses," Historical New York City Crime Data, data table (2000–2019), https://www1.nyc.gov/assets/nypd/downloads/pdf/analysis_and_planning/historical-crime-data/seven-major-felony-offenses-by-precinct-2000-2019.pdf (the seven offenses are murder and non-negligent manslaughter, rape, robbery, felony assault, burglary, grand larceny, and grand larceny of a motor vehicle).

32. New York Police Department, "Seven Major Felony Offenses."

33. See New York Police Department, "Non-Seven Major Felony Offenses," n. 303 (data table 2000–2019), https://www1.nyc.gov/assets/nypd/downloads/pdf/analysis_and_planning/historical-crime-data/non-seven-major-felony-offenses-by-precinct-2000-2019.pdf.

34. New York Police Department, "Non-Seven Major Felony Offenses."

35. Note that one of the precincts included among these fifteen (the 78th Precinct) had its boundaries slightly adjusted in 2011.

36. See New York Police Department, "Non-Seven Major Felony Offenses," n. 302.

37. New York Police Department, "Seven Major Felony Offenses."

38. New York Police Department, "Seven Major Felony Offenses."

39. New York Police Department, "Non-Seven Major Felony Offenses."

40. New York Police Department, "Non-Seven Major Felony Offenses."

41. New York Police Department, "Supplementary Homicide Report," https://www1.nyc.gov/site/nypd/stats/reports-analysis/homicide.page.

42. See appendix to "Stop and Frisk in the de Blasio Era," https://www.nyclu.org/sites/default/files/field_documents/20190314_nyclu_stopfrisk_appendices_onlineonly.pdf.

43. See Chicago Police Department, *2020 Annual Report*, 50–52, https://home. chicagopolice.org/wp-content/uploads/Annual_Report_2020.pdf.

44. *Terry v. Ohio*, 392 US 1 (1968).

45. "Floyd, et al. v. City of New York, et al.," Center for Constitutional Rights, https://ccrjustice.org/home/what-we-do/our-cases/ floyd-et-al-v-city-new-york-et-al.

46. "Floyd, et al. v. City of New York, et al."

47. Joel Rose, "De Blasio Drops Appeal of 'Stop and Frisk,'" NPR, January 30, 2014, https://www.npr.org/2014/01/30/268964572/ de-blasio-drops-appeal-of-stop-and-frisk.

48. "Floyd, et al. v. City of New York, et al.," Opinion, Center for Constitutional Rights, https://ccrjustice.org/sites/default/files/assets/Floyd-Liability-Opinion-8-12-13.pdf.

49. See Rafael A. Mangual, "Wrong-Footing the NYPD," *City Journal*, December 22, 2017; Ashley Southall, "Right to Know Is Now the Law. Here's What That Means," *New York Times*, October 19, 2018.

50. Right to Know Act—Requiring the NYPD to develop and provide guidance for its officers on obtaining consent to search individuals, Int 0541-2014, New York City Council, enacted January 19, 2018, https://legistar.council.nyc.gov/LegislationDetail. aspx?ID=2015555&GUID=652280A4-40A6-44C4-A6AF-8EF4717BD8D6.

51. *Florida v. Bostick*, 501 US 429 (1991).

52. *United States v. Drayton* (01-631) 536 US 194 (2002), 231 F.3d 787, reversed and remanded.

53. Peter L. Zimroth (NYPD Monitor), *Seventh Report of the Independent Monitor*, December 13, 2017, http://nypdmonitor.org/wp-content/uploads/2017/12/2017-12-13-FloydLigonDavis-Monitor-Seventh-Report_EAST_80301353_1.pdf.

54. Zimroth, *Seventh Report of the Independent Monitor*, 41.

55. Zimroth, *Seventh Report of the Independent Monitor*, 42.

## CHAPTER SEVEN: RACE: THE ELEPHANT IN THE ROOM

1. Wesley Lowery, "Aren't More White People Than Black People Killed by Police? Yes, but No," *Washington Post*, July 11, 2016.

2. "Report to the United Nations on Racial Disparities in the US Criminal Justice System," Sentencing Project, March 2018, https://www.sentencingproject.org/publications/un-report-on-racial-disparities.

3. "Report to the United Nations on Racial Disparities in the US Criminal Justice System."

4. John Stuart Mill, "Of the Liberty of Thought and Discussion," *On Liberty* (John W. Parker and Son, West Strand, 1859).

5. Radley Balko, "There's Overwhelming Evidence" (emphasis added).

6. David Weisburd and Malay K. Majmundar, eds., *Proactive Policing: Effects on Crime and Communities* (National Academies Press, 2018), 252.

7. Weisburd and Majmundar, *Proactive Policing: Effects on Crime and Communities*, 253.

8. Merriam-Webster's online dictionary of the English language provides a good example of the common understanding of the term: "a belief that race is a fundamental determinant of human traits and capacities and that racial differences produce an inherent superiority of a particular race." Merriam-Webster.com Dictionary, s.v. "racism," accessed January 20, 2022.

9. NEPM Newsroom, "Tensions High During Pre-Election Demonstrations in Northampton," New England Public Media, November 2, 2020, https://www.nepm.org/post/tensions-high-during-pre-election-demonstrations-northampton#stream/0.

10. Weisburd and Majmundar, *Proactive Policing: Effects on Crime and Communities*, 298 n. 333.

11. National Research Council, *The Growth of Incarceration in the United States: Exploring Causes and Consequences,* Edited by Jeremy Travis, Bruce Western, and Steve Redburn (National Academies Press, 2014), 97.

12. National Research Council, *The Growth of Incarceration in the United States*, 98.

13. Cassia C. Spohn, "Thirty Years of the Sentencing Reform: The Quest for a Racially Neutral Sentencing Process," *Criminal Justice* 3 (2000): 427–501.

14. See Fryer, "An Empirical Analysis of Racial Differences in Police Use of Force," n. 299.

15. Alma Cohen and Crystal S. Yang, "Judicial Politics and Sentencing Decisions," *American Economic Journal: Economic Policy* 11, no. 1 (February 2019): 160–191.

16. 543 US 220 (2005).

17. See Cohen and Yang, "Judicial Politics and Sentencing Decisions," 3 n. 342.

18. Cohen and Yang, "Judicial Politics and Sentencing Decisions," 3 n. 342.

19. Cohen and Yang, "Judicial Politics and Sentencing Decisions," 2.

20. See, for example, John Pfaff, *Locked In: The True Causes of Mass Incarceration and How to Achieve Real Reform* (Basic Books, 2017), 33: "That drug crime admissions [to prison] rose more rapidly during a time of rising violence suggests that at least some of these drug admissions, maybe many, were pretextual attacks on violence. In other words, some . . . were targeted as a way to punish more serious—but harder-to-prove—violent crime."). See also Barry Latzer, *The Rise and Fall of Violent Crime in America* (Encounter Books, 2016), 182 (noting that through the 1990s, "In many respects, the war on drugs was a second front in the war on crime in the United States") and 253 (noting that "Incarceration for drug crimes, which, strictly speaking, are not considered crimes of violence, nevertheless contributed to the decline in violent crime, *given the propensity of the cocaine offenders to engage in violence*" [emphasis added]).

21. FBI, *Crime in the United States,* 2018, "Clearances." https://ucr.fbi.gov/crime-in-the-u.s/2018/crime-in-the-u.s.-2018/topic-pages/clearances.

22. FBI, *Crime in the United States,* 2018.

23. See Pfaff, *Locked In,* 33 n. 347.

24. Kevin Rector, "2017 Homicide Data Provide Insight into Baltimore's Gun Wars, Police Say," *Baltimore Sun,* January 3, 2018.

25. Alpher, Durose, and Markman, "2018 Update on Prisoner Recidivism."

26. See Latzer, *The Rise and Fall of Violent Crime in America,* 177, 180 n. 347.

27. Anti-Drug Abuse Act of 1986, HR 5484, 99th Congress (1985–1986), https://www.congress.gov/bill/99th-congress/house-bill/5484/actions.

28. See Donna Murch, "Crack in Los Angeles: Crisis, Militarization, and Black Response to the Late Twentieth-Century War on Drugs," *Journal of American History* 102, no. 1 (June 2015): "The progressive California congressman Ronald V. Dellums, along with fifteen other members of the Congressional Black Caucus, actually co-sponsored the bill, which resulted in the 100:1 disparity for crack versus powder cocaine in federal drug cases, resulting in the disproportionate incarceration of large numbers of African American offenders."

29. See Michael Javen Fortner, "The Carceral State and the Crucible of Black Politics: An Urban History of the Rockefeller Drug Laws," *Studies in American*

*Political Development* 27, no. 1 (April 2013): 13–35; see also Fortner, *Black Silent Majority: The Rockefeller Drug Laws and the Politics of Punishment* (Cambridge, MA: Harvard University Press, 2015).

30. Charles Murray, *Losing Ground: American Social Policy, 1950–1980* (Basic Books, 1984), 117.

31. See Latzer, *The Rise and Fall of Violent Crime in America*, 178 n. 347.

32. Patrick Sharkey, *Uneasy Peace: The Great Crime Decline, the Renewal of City Life, and the Next War on Violence* (W. W. Norton, 2018), 12–13.

33. Sharkey, *Uneasy Peace*, 69–70.

34. Sharkey, *Uneasy Peace*, 69.

35. See Rafael A. Mangual, "Turning away from Success," *City Journal*, April 11, 2019.

36. See, for example, Rafael A. Mangual, "'Justice' for Whom?" *City Journal*, March 20, 2019; Rafael A. Mangual, "The Troubling Agenda of LA's New 'Progressive' Prosecutor and Fellow 'Reformers,'" *The Hill*, December 10, 2020.

37. John Gramlich, "Black Imprisonment Rate in the U.S. Has Fallen by a Third since 2006," Pew Research Center, May 6, 2020, https://www.pewresearch.org/fact-tank/2020/05/06/share-of-black-white-hispanic-americans-in-prison-2018-vs-2006.

38. Gramlich, "Black Imprisonment Rate in the U.S. Has Fallen."

39. Gramlich, "Black Imprisonment Rate in the U.S. Has Fallen."

40. United States Sentencing Commission, *Report to the Congress: Impact of the Fair Sentencing Act of 2010*, August 2015, 27, https://www.ussc.gov/sites/default/files/pdf/news/congressional-testimony-and-reports/drug-topics/201507_RtC_Fair-Sentencing-Act.pdf#page=27.

41. Jim Parsons et al., "End of An Era? The Impact of Drug Law Reform in New York City," Vera Institute of Justice, January 2015, https://www.vera.org/publications/end-of-an-era-the-impact-of-drug-law-reform-in-new-york-city.

42. See, for example, Jenny Gross and John Eligon, "Minneapolis City Council Votes to Remove $8 Million from Police Budget," *New York Times*, December 10, 2020; Dana Rubinstein and Jeffery C. Mays, "Nearly $1 Billion Is Shifted from Police in Budget That Pleases No One," *New York Times,* June 30, 2020; Jon Regardie, "What We Know So Far about the LAPD's Dramatic Cost-Cutting Measures," *Los Angeles Magazine*, November 20, 2020.

43. Alexa Lardieri, "Gov. Andrew Cuomo Signs 10-Bill Police Reform Package into Law," *US News and World Report*, June 12, 2020.

44. Steve Janoski, "New Jersey Issues Sweeping Changes on How Police Can Use Force," *North Jersey*, December 21, 2020, https://www.northjersey.com/story/news/new-jersey/2020/12/21/nj-police-force-de-escalation/3906841001.

45. See, for example, William J. Bratton, *Broken Windows Is Not Broken: The NYPD Response to the Inspector General's Report on Quality of Life Enforcement*, New York Police Department, https://www1.nyc.gov/assets/nypd/downloads/pdf/broken_windows_is_not_broken.pdf (wherein then-NYPD Commissioner William Bratton cites the crime declines of the 1990s and early 2000s in defense of broken windows policing).

## CONCLUSION

1. Rafael A. Mangual, "Everything You Don't Know about Mass Incarceration," *City Journal*, Summer 2019, https://www.city-journal.org/mass-incarceration (showing that releasing all those incarcerated for drug offenses, larceny, and motor vehicle theft, fraud, other property offenses, DUI, other public order offenses, and other unspecified offenses would still leave the US with an incarceration rate more than double that of the United Kingdom and quadruple that of Germany).

2. Rafael A. Mangual, "The Homicide Spike Is Real," *New York Times*, January 19, 2021.

3. Larry Celona and Kenneth Garger, "Three Charged in Killing of Bronx Father Gunned Down while Walking with Daughter," *New York Post*, July 17, 2020.

4. Jim Patrick, "Three Gang-Bangers Who Shot and Killed a Man Walking with His 6-Year-Old Daughter Have Been Arrested," Law Enforcement Today, July 18, 2020, https://www.lawenforcementtoday.com/nypd-arrests-three-men-for-killing-of-man-walking-with-6-year-old-daughter.

## APPENDIX 1: TESTIMONY BEFORE THE US SENATE COMMITTEE ON THE JUDICIARY'S SUBCOMMITTEE ON CRIMINAL JUSTICE AND COUNTERTERRORISM

1. Eric Kaufmann, *The Social Construction of Racism in the United States*, Manhattan Institute for Policy Research, April 2021.

2. Eli Yokley, "Poll: Voters More Worried by Violence Against Police Than Police Brutality," Morning Consult, July 11, 2016 (see crosstabs).

3. Frank Edwards, Hedwig Lee, and Michael Esposito, "Risk of Being Killed by Police Use of Force in the United States by Age, Race–Ethnicity, and Sex," *Proceedings of the National Academy of Sciences* (2019); see also Alex Berezow,

"Most Dangerous Drivers Ranked by State, Age, Race, and Sex," American Council on Science and Health, August 10, 2018 (showing that the traffic death rate for Black people is about 13 per 100,000).

4. Lifetime odds of death for selected causes, United States, 2018, NSC.org.

5. Rich Morin and Andrew Mercer, "A Closer Look at Police Officers Who Have Fired Their Weapon on Duty," FactTank, Pew Research Center, February 8, 2017.

6. Rafael A. Mangual, "Police Use of Force and the Practical Limits of Popular Reform Proposals: A Response to Rizer and Mooney," *Federalist Society Review* 21 (2020): 129.

7. *Crime in the United States, 2018*: Table 29 (Estimated Number of Arrests), Federal Bureau of Investigation.

8. Mangual, "Police Use of Force," n. 5.

9. William P. Bozeman et al., "Injuries Associated with Police Use of Force," *Journal of Trauma and Acute Care Surgery* 84 (March 2018): 466.

10. Bozeman et al., "Injuries Associated with Police Use of Force," 466.

11. Bozeman et al., "Injuries Associated with Police Use of Force," 466.

12. See NYPD Force Dashboard (start date, Wednesday, January 1, 2020; end date, Thursday, December 31, 2020).

13. See NYPD Force Dashboard.

14. See Use of Force Data Tables, NYPD (see quarterly incidents by force category).

15. German Lopez, "2020's Historic Surge in Murders, Explained," Vox, March 25, 2021.

16. Alexia Cooper and Erica L. Smith, "Homicide Trends in the United States, 1980–2008," Bureau of Justice Statistics (November 2011).

17. Adam Ferrise, "'It's Like War Numbers': Cleveland Endures Worst Homicide Rate in Recent History in 2020," Cleveland.com, January 1, 2021.

18. Libor Jany, "Minneapolis Violent Crimes Soared in 2020 amid Pandemic, Protests," *Minneapolis Star Tribune* (Feb. 6, 2021).

19. See Jennifer Edwards Baker, "Cincinnati Police Updates Council on 2020 Crime Stats, Record-High Homicides," Fox 19, January 20, 2021; Kala Kachmar, Lucas Aulbach, and Jonathan Bullington, "170-Plus Killings and Few Answers: Louisville Besieged by Record Homicides and Gun Violence," *Courier Journal*, January 5, 2021.

20. See Crime and Enforcement Activity Reports, NYPD (each of the reports from 2008 to 2020 break down the percentages of shooting victims by race).

21. A robust body of research suggests that replenishing departments can and will have significant crime-reduction effects. Some examples: Economists Jonathan Klick and Alexander Tabarrok found a strong causal connection between police presence and crime, showing that the latter declined when the former was boosted. (See "Using Terror Alert Levels to Estimate the Effect of Police on Crime," *Journal of Law and Economics* 48, no. 1 [April 2005]: 267–279.) In another study, Klick, along with criminologist John MacDonald and law professor Ben Grunwald, found that an increase in police patrols around the University of Pennsylvania "decreased crime in adjacent city blocks by 43%–73%." (See "The Effect of Private Police on Crime: Evidence from a Geographic Regression Discontinuity Design," Journal of the Royal Statistical Society 179, no. 3 [June 2016]: 831–846.) Criminologist Aaron Chalfin, along with law professor Justin McCrary, found "reduced victim costs of $1.63 for each additional dollar spent on police in 2010, implying that U.S. cities are under-policed." (See "Are U.S. Cities Underpoliced? Theory and Evidence," Review of Economics and Statistics 100, no. 1 [March 2018]: 167–186.)

22. Patrick Sharkey and Michael Friedson, "The Impact of the Homicide Decline on Life Expectancy of African American Males," *Demography* 56, no. 2 (March 5, 2019): 645–663.

23. Patrick Sharkey, *Uneasy Peace: The Great Crime Decline, the Renewal of City Life, and the Next War on Violence* (W. W. Norton, 2018).

24. Lawrence W. Sherman, James W. Shaw, and Dennis P. Rogan, "The Kansas City Gun Experiment," National Institute of Justice, Research Brief (January 1995).

25. Charles Fain Lehman, "Policing without the Police? A Review of the Evidence," Manhattan Institute for Policy Research, Report, May 2021.

26. Lehman, "Policing without the Police?" 7 (internal citations omitted).

27. Jerry H. Ratcliffe, "Policing and Public Health Calls for Service in Philadelphia," *Crime Science* 10, no. 5 (2021).

28. Ratcliffe, "Policing and Public Health Calls for Service in Philadelphia."

29. See, e.g., Rafael A. Mangual, "MI Responds: Five Ideas for a More Sensible Approach to Police Reform," Manhattan Institute for Policy Research, June 12, 2020.

## APPENDIX 2: STATEMENT TO THE PRESIDENT'S COMMISSION ON LAW ENFORCEMENT: WORKING GROUP ON RESPECT FOR LAW ENFORCEMENT

1. For a sampling of this work, see the following reports, essays, and columns: Rafael A. Mangual, "Police Use of Force and the Practical Limits of Popular Reform Proposals: A Response to Rizer and Mooney," *Federalist Society Review* 21 (2020): 128; Rafael A. Mangual, *Reforming New York's Bail Reform: A Public Safety-Minded Proposal*, Manhattan Institute for Policy Research, March 2020; Rafael A. Mangual, *Issues 2020: Mass Decarceration Will Increase Violent Crime*, Manhattan Institute for Policy Research, September 2019; Rafael A. Mangual, "'Equity' before Security," *City Journal*, March 15, 2018; Rafael A. Mangual, "Fathers, Families, and Incarceration," *City Journal*, Winter 2020; Rafael A. Mangual, "Bloomberg Wants to Be Strong on Guns and Soft on Crime," *Washington Post*, November 24, 2019; Rafael A. Mangual, "Biden Should Be Proud of His Record on Crime," *Wall Street Journal*, April 24, 2019; Rafael A. Mangual, "No, Philly Doesn't Need to Cure Poverty to Reduce Crime," *Philadelphia Inquirer*, June 24, 2019.

2. Matthew Hendrickson and Alison Martin, "Baby Waved, Smiled at Men Right before They Killed Her Mother, Prosecutors Say," *Chicago Sun-Times*, May 30, 2019.

3. Ali Watkins, "Man Who Shot Up a Bronx Precinct Was 'Tired of Police Officers,'" *New York Times*, February 10, 2020.

4. Rafael A. Mangual, "With Good Reason, Indeed," *Law and Liberty*, March 17, 2020.

5. Office for National Statistics, *Population Estimates for the UK, England and Wales, Scotland, and Northern Ireland: Mid-2018.*

6. Office for National Statistics, *Homicide in England and Wales: Year Ending March 2018.*

7. See Chicago Police Department, 2018 Annual Report; and CMAP Illinois, *Community Data Snapshots.*

8. "Baltimore Homicides," *Baltimore Sun.*

9. Bureau of Justice Statistics, *Felony Sentences in State Courts.*

10. Danielle Kaeble, *Time Served in State Prison, 2016*, Bureau of Justice Statistics, November 2018.

11. Jennifer Bronson and E. Ann Carson, *Prisoners in 2017, Bureau of Justice Statistics*, April 2019.

12. Michelle Alexander, *The New Jim Crow: Mass Incarceration in the Age of Colorblindness* (New Press, 2010).

13. Ava DuVernay, *13th*, Netflix (2016).

14. Danielle Kaeble, *Time Served in State Prison, 2016*, Bureau of Justice Statistics, November 2018.

15. Mariel Alper, Matthew R. Durose, and Joshua Markman, *2018 Update on Prisoner Recidivism: A 9-Year Follow-up Period* (2004–2014), Bureau of Justice Statistics, May 2018.

16. See Taylor Pendergrass, *We Can Cut Mass Incarceration by 50 Percent*, ACLU, July 12, 2019.

17. "91 Percent of Americans Support Criminal Justice Reform, ACLU Polling Finds," ACLU press release, November 16, 2017.

18. German Lopez, "Want to End Mass Incarceration? This Poll Should Worry You," Vox (September 7, 2016).

19. Dante de Blasio, "My Dad Gave Me 'the Talk.' When Someone Called Police, I Felt the Fear," *USA Today*, July 1, 2019.

20. See Mangual, "Police Use of Force," 129.

21. Crime in the United States, 2018: Table 74 (Full-Time Law Enforcement Employees), Federal Bureau of Investigation. Note: This number likely undercounts the total number of law enforcement officers operating within the US, given that in many parts of the country—particularly in rural, exurban, and suburban areas—many public safety operations use part-time and reserve officers.

22. Crime in the United States, 2018: Table 29 (Estimated Number of Arrests), Federal Bureau of Investigation.

23. *Contacts between Police and the Public, 2015*, Bureau of Justice Statistics, October 2018.

24. W. P. Bozeman et al., "Injuries Associated with Police Use of Force," *Journal of Trauma and Acute Care Surgery* 84 (March 2018).

25. Matthew Desmond, Andrew V. Papachristos, and David S. Kirk, "Police Violence and Citizen Crime Reporting in the Black Community," *American Sociological Review* 81, no. 5 (2016): 857–876.

26. Eli Yokley, "Poll: Voters More Worried by Violence against Police Than Police Brutality," Morning Consult, July 11, 2016.

27. Frank Edwards, Hedwig Lee, and Michael Esposito, "Risk of Being Killed by Police Use of Force in the United States by Age, Race–Ethnicity, and Sex," *Proceedings of the National Academy of Sciences* (2019).

28. "Lifetime Odds of Death for Selected Causes, United States," 2018, NSC.org.

29. See, for example, Corinne Riddell et al., "Comparison of Rates of Firearm and Nonfirearm Homicide and Suicide in Black and White Non-Hispanic Men, by U.S. State," *Annals of Internal Medicine* 168, no. 10 (2018) (finding that "In 2016, non-Hispanic black men were nearly 10.4 times more likely than non-Hispanic white men to die by homicide in the United States").

30. See *Citywide Crime Statistics: Compstat Report Covering the Week 7/6/2020 through 7/12/2020* (copy on file with author).

31. See *Citywide Crime Statistics*.

32. See *Citywide Crime Statistics*.

33. Sergio Hernandez et al., "Tracking Covid-19 Cases in the US," CNN.com (updated Jul. 20, 2020).

34. "Coronavirus News: NYPD Has 5,600 Officers out Sick, 5 Deaths," WABC-TV, March 31, 2020.

# ABOUT THE AUTHOR

**RAFAEL A. MANGUAL** is a senior fellow and head of research for policing and public safety at the Manhattan Institute for Policy Research—the think tank renowned for its scholarship on the "broken windows" theory of policing in the 1980s and 1990s, and for its role in the transformation of New York City into one of the world's safest and most attractive urban centers. He is also a contributing editor of the Institute's flagship quarterly magazine, *City Journal*.

Rafael began his career in policy journalism shortly after graduating from law school, and has since become a fixture in the nation's ongoing debates about crime, policing, and incarceration. He has published a number of policy papers and columns for broad public consumption in a wide variety of outlets, including *The New York Times*, *The Wall Street Journal*, and the *Washington Post*. Rafael regularly appears on national and local television and radio programs, and he is a regular speaker at policy conferences and on college and law school campuses.

A graduate of the City University of New York's Baruch College and DePaul University's College of Law, Rafael lives in New York City with his wife and their children.